POLITICS AND THE ACADEMY:
ARNOLD TOYNBEE AND THE KORAES CHAIR

POLITICS
AND THE
ACADEMY

Arnold Toynbee and the
Koraes Chair

RICHARD CLOGG

FRANK CASS
in association with
The Centre of Contemporary Greek Studies,
King's College London

First published 1986 in Great Britain by
FRANK CASS AND COMPANY LIMITED
Gainsborough House, 11 Gainsborough Road,
London E11 1RS, England
in association with
The Centre of Contemporary Greek Studies,
King's College London

and in the United States of America by
FRANK CASS AND COMPANY LIMITED
c/o Biblio Distribution Centre
81 Adams Drive, P.O. Box 327, Totowa, NJ 07511

British Library Cataloguing in Publication Data

Clogg, Richard
    Politics and the academy : Arnold Toynbee and
    the Koraes Chair.
    1. Toynbee, Arnold, *1889-1975* ——Resignation from
    office   2. King's College, London
I. Title
    378.421'32   LF434.T6

ISBN 0-7146-3290-2

This study first appeared in a Special Issue of *Middle Eastern Studies*, Vol.
21, No. 4, published by Frank Cass & Co. Ltd.

Printed in England by Specialised Printing Services Ltd.
40, Chigwell Lane, Loughton, Essex IG10 3TZ

Contents

PREFACE   vi

1 THE ESTABLISHMENT OF THE CHAIR   1

2 THE ELECTION   22

3 THE CONTROVERSY   53

4 THE AFTERMATH   108

APPENDIX: TOYNBEE'S LETTER TO THE TIMES OF
3 JANUARY 1924   116

Preface

The history of academic institutions is seldom written *'wie es eigentlich gewesen'*. It is characteristic that the two histories of King's College, London,[1] do not dwell on one of the great academic *causes célèbres* of the early twentieth century, which had something of the public *éclat* occasioned by the college's dismissal in the mid-nineteenth century of the Reverend Professor F.D. Maurice for having the temerity to question the dogma of the eternal punishment of the wicked. This was the furious controversy that developed in the early 1920s between Arnold Toynbee, the first incumbent of the Koraes Chair, and the subscribers who had put up the money for the endowment and who enjoyed the support of a powerful group in the King's professoriate, a confrontation that ceased only with Toynbee's resignation.

The establishment in 1918 of the Koraes Chair of Modern Greek and Byzantine History, Language and Literature at King's College, London, arose out of the friendship of Ronald Burrows, Principal of the College between 1913 and 1920, with the Greek statesman Eleftherios Venizelos, Prime Minister of Greece 1910–15 and 1917–20 (and subsequently 1928–32). Venizelos not only arranged the voting in the Greek Parliament of an annual (if short-lived) subsidy for the new department, but contributed directly to the endowment of the Koraes Chair, while it was the knowledge that the establishment of the chair enjoyed his blessing that encouraged the markedly Venizelist Greek community in Britain to raise the bulk of the endowment. The first holder of the chair, Arnold Toynbee, fresh from his wartime service as a specialist in Near Eastern affairs for the British government, was appointed for an initial five-year term in 1919.

Much of Toynbee's tenure of the chair, coinciding as it did with Greece's disastrous entanglement in Asia Minor, was to be marked by fierce controversy. This was largely occasioned by a series of articles that he wrote on the Greek–Turkish conflict when, for nine months in 1921, on leave of absence from the university, he served as a special correspondent for the *Manchester Guardian*. In these dispatches he was highly critical of the behaviour of the Greek army in Asia Minor. On his return he wrote, at remarkable speed, a brilliant analysis of the origins and progress of the conflict between Orthodox Christian and Muslim civilization in Asia Minor, *The Western Question in Greece and Turkey: a Study in the Contact of Civilisations* (London 1922). In this he repeated the charge that the Greek forces in Asia Minor had committed atrocities, argued that the Greek position in Asia Minor was untenable and concluded that the Greeks had demonstrated 'the same unfitness as the Turks for governing a mixed population'. In the preface he acknowledged that it was likely to be 'painful to Greeks and "Philhellenes" that information and reflections unfavourable to Greece should have been published by the first occupant of the Korais Chair', and it was inevitable that the publication of the book a few months before the catastrophic defeat of the Greek armies in Asia Minor should have grievously offended the Greek subscribers to the Koraes Chair endowment. From early 1923 the donors, grouped in the Subscribers' Committee, made vigorous representations to the university, holding that Toynbee's activities as Koraes Professor were incompatible with his continued tenure of the chair. As a consequence of the ensuing pressures Toynbee resigned the chair with effect from July 1924, when his initial five-year term came to an end.

The present study[2] covers in some detail the negotiations leading up to the foundation of the chair, which afford an insight into what Principal Burrows and some at least of the subscribers saw as its essential purposes; the search for a suitable candidate; the election of Toynbee and the ensuing furore. I have concentrated very much on the academic aspects of the controversy and have discussed Toynbee's writings, journalistic and academic, on Greek–Turkish relations only in so far as some knowledge of these is necessary to an understanding of the academic controversy that ensued. Toynbee was the compiler of the Government Blue Book on *The Treatment of Armenians in the Ottoman Empire* (London 1916), an undertaking during which, as he himself put it, he had learned 'nearly all that there is to be learnt to the discredit of the Turkish nation and of their rule over other peoples'. He was also the author of *The Murderous Tyranny of the Turks* (London 1917), a tract replete with anti-Turkish rhetoric of the 'where Ottoman rule has spread civilization has perished' variety. The process whereby he was to emerge as the harsh critic of Greek rule in Asia Minor and the committed champion of Kemalist Turkey can be studied in Toynbee's voluminous contemporary writings on Near Eastern affairs[3] and, above all in *The Western Question* itself.[4]

It is possible to document this extraordinary story in considerable detail, for a number of collections of papers, reflecting the views of all the major protagonists in the controversy, survive. Moreover, these records are sufficiently detailed to enable much of what the Greeks term the *paraskinia*, the things behind the scenes, to be reconstructed. One of the reasons for this would appear to lie in the fact that whereas telephones obviously existed in the early 1920s (King's College at that time had all of two lines) they were clearly not yet used for the transaction of academic business, and the conduct of academic intrigue, in the way that they would be now. Indeed, one of the principal protagonists in the story, Joannes Gennadius, the Greek minister in London, even had a strong aversion to the use of the typewriter.[5] Whatever the reason, the historian has cause to be grateful for the fact that there is certainly no shortage of documentation.

The principal protagonist in the dispute, Arnold Toynbee, not only meticulously preserved all his papers relating to the chair but also annotated them. In a letter to me of 27 July 1974 he wrote that he would be happy to lend these to me: 'there is nothing confidential about them, as far as I am concerned, but, though they are now ancient history for me, they do have a permanent interest because of their bearing on the perennial question of academic freedom'. Fifty years earlier, on 5 January 1924, he had written to his principal antagonist within the college, Professor R.W. Seton-Watson, to say that he personally had 'always wished that full public light should be thrown upon the whole history of the chair and of my tenure of it'. There is some mystery about the present whereabouts of the papers of Principal Burrows without whose drive and enthusiasm for the Greek, and in particular the Venizelist, cause the Koraes Chair would never have been established. In his *Propagande et pressions en politique internationale: La Grèce et ses revendications à la Conférence de la Paix (1919–1920)*,[6] Professor Dimitri Kitsikis states that Burrows's personal archives were deposited by his widow, Mrs Una Burrows, in the Greek Legation in London where they were extensively used by George Glasgow in his *Ronald Burrows: a Memoir* (London 1924). There is, however, now no trace of these papers either in the Greek Embassy in London or in the Ministry of Foreign Affairs in Athens. This is unfortunate but not so serious from the point of view of this study as it might have been, for Mrs Burrows presented those of her husband's papers bearing particularly on the establishment of the Koraes Chair to King's College. The college appears promptly to have mislaid them, but they presumably came to light subsequently, for a substantial body of material relating to the foundation of the chair is preserved in the college archives. Given the federal structure of the University of London, the controversy arising from Toynbee's tenure of the chair was as much a university as a college matter, perhaps more so. Useful material relating to the university's deliberations on the matter is preserved in the university's archives. Important material also survives among the papers of the Subscribers' Committee which was established by the Greek benefactors of the Koraes Chair, and of its chairman, Joannes Gennadius, the scholar diplomat who was Greek minister in London at the time of the establishment of the chair. Relevant material is also preserved among the papers of Professor R.W. Seton-Watson, Masaryk Professor of Central European History in the School of Slavonic Studies, which during this period remained a part of King's College.

Toynbee's experiences during his tenure of the Koraes Chair have a certain contemporary relevance in that they highlight some of the dangers inherent in the tendency manifest in recent years for British universities to look to external sources of funding when faced with financial stringency. Particularly in the case of 'minority' subjects, recourse is had to funding from foreign governments. Moreover, the increasing impoverishment of the universities has to a degree coincided with a growing concern on the part of newer nations, particularly those with the financial resources to match, to project a favourable image by encouraging the development of the study of their languages and cultures through the endowment of chairs, departments and centres in the universities. While it would clearly be an exaggeration to argue that a particular branch of study at a university is compromised by the mere fact that it is subsidized in part or in whole by funds deriving from a foreign government, none the less the dangers inherent in such arrangements are self evident, as that great scholar journalist, William Miller, was well aware when he was approached to fill the Koraes Chair as the favoured candidate of Principal Burrows and Eleftherios Venizelos. There have already been indications that the acceptance of external sources of funding has, in certain cases, had thoroughly undesirable consequences in circumscribing that unfettered spirit of enquiry that lies at the heart of the concept of the university.[7]

It is a pleasant duty to acknowledge the assistance of a number of individuals in the preparation of this study for publication. Adrianne Savage processed the manuscript with great efficiency. Patricia Methven, the archivist of King's College, London; Joan Gibbs, the archivist of the University of London; Helen Langley of the Department of Western Manuscripts of the Bodleian Library, Oxford; and Mrs Sophie Papageorgiou, librarian of the Gennadius Library of the American School of Classical Studies in Athens were helpful in making available material in their custody. Mrs Veronica Toynbee kindly granted access to her husband's correspondence relating to the Koraes Chair, as did the Principal of the University of London, Dr William Taylor, to materials in the university archives, and the Secretary of King's College, Myles Tempany, to the relevant sections of the college archives. Mr Tempany's predecessor, Hugh Patterson, was also helpful in this respect. Hugh Seton-Watson generously granted me access to the papers of his father, R.W. Seton-Watson, as did Dr Beata Panagopoulou, the Director of the Gennadius Library of the American School of Classical Studies, to the papers of Joannes Gennadius. Professor J.G. Joachim kindly alerted me to the existence of the Gennadius papers relating to the Koraes Chair. The archivist of the Venizelos Archive in the Benaki Museum, Athens, enabled me to consult Principal Burrows' correspondence with Eleftherios Venizelos. Victoria Solomonidis helpfully made enquiries as to the present whereabouts of the papers of Principal Burrows and made available material from the archives of the Ministry of Foreign Affairs in Athens relating to Arnold Toynbee's travels in Asia Minor in 1921. Ian Martin kindly provided information about Nicholas ('Eumo') Eumorfopoulos' career at University College. Professor George Forrest promptly identified the passage from Polybius with which Toynbee wished to end his letter to *The Times* of 3 January 1924. Donald Nicol, the present holder of the Koraes Chair, has read the manuscript and made a number of useful comments, as has Professor P.J. Marshall, Rhodes Professor of Imperial History at King's College.

Should any profits arise from this publication, then it seems only fitting that they should be devoted to the purchase of books for the Burrows Library at King's College in memory of the various protagonists in the controversy, all of whom, in their different ways, were deeply committed to the promotion of Byzantine and Modern Greek Studies.

RICHARD CLOGG
Department of Byzantine and Modern Greek Studies,
King's College, University of London

NOTES

1. F.J.C. Hearnshaw, *A Centenary History of King's College London* (London, 1928) and Gordon Huelin, *King's College London: a history commemorating the 150th anniversary of the foundation of the College* (London, 1978). Hearnshaw, although he does not mention

Toynbee by name, has some pertinent remarks to make about the establishment of the chair. Adverting to the establishment of four new departments in the college during the First World War, namely Slavonic, Spanish, Portuguese and Modern Greek, he noted:

the fact that governments and politicians were interested in these modern linguistic chairs had advantages in securing money and promises of money for their inauguration and maintenance – although the actual payment of foreign government grants proved to be liable to frequent interruption by revolution or change of administration. It carried with it, however, the grave disadvantage that the holder of these subsidized seats found his academic freedom compromised. He was expected to teach what was agreeable to his patrons. The first holder of the Korais Chair, for instance, appointed in 1919, became embroiled on political grounds with the Greek government and the Greek committee in London, and his position became an intolerable one. He resigned in 1924; and before a successor was elected the conditions of tenure had to be radically altered (op.cit. pp. 466–7).

2. A brief account of the establishment of the Koraes Chair is to be included in the proceedings of the First Anglo-Greek Historical Colloquium, Salonica 1983, to be published by the Institute for Balkan Studies.

3. These are conveniently listed in S. Fiona Morton, *A Bibliography of Arnold J. Toynbee* (Oxford, 1980) pp. 53–65.

4. Toynbee has some interesting reflections on this period in his *Acquaintances* (Oxford, 1967) pp. 242ff. See also Elie Kedourie, 'The Chatham House Version' in *The Chatham House Version and other Middle Eastern Studies* (London, 1970) pp. 351–462 and Norman Ravitch, 'The Armenian catastrophe' in *Encounter* (November 1981) pp. 69–84.

5. A.A. Pallis, *Xenitemenoi Ellines. Aftoviographiko khroniko* (Athens, 1954) p. 94.

6. (Paris, 1963) p. 459.

7. Some of these have been highlighted in Peter Bradley, *Undue Influence: Pressures on the Universities*, Centre for Contemporary Studies, Occasional Paper No. 2 (1983).

1. The Establishment of the Chair

Any study of the foundation of the Koraes Chair at King's College, London, must begin with Ronald Burrows, Principal of the college between 1913 and his death in 1920. From the outset, he was the driving force behind its establishment. Burrows was born in 1867 and educated at Charterhouse and Christ Church, Oxford. With a first class degree in Mods and Greats (Greek, Latin and Ancient Philosophy), Burrows' first academic appointment was as assistant to Gilbert Murray, Professor of Greek in the University of Glasgow, a connection that was to have important consequences in the story of the Koraes Chair. Burrows was subsequently appointed Professor of Greek at University College, Cardiff, and later at the University of Manchester. During these years, Burrows, a Christian socialist, developed a strong interest in modern Greece. In the course of his topographical researches in the Peloponnese he was impressed by the vigour with which the Greeks conducted their politics and was fond of contrasting this with the apathy he had encountered in the municipal politics of Glasgow. At one local election in Pylos he had come across the local citizenry, 'with many bands and banners', electing a town council of 15 members. The voters' roll contained 1200 names and there was a total of 127 candidates.[1]

During his time at Manchester he demonstrated a keen interest in the Balkan wars of 1912 and 1913 and his enthusiasm for the Greek cause found expression in his 'Song of the Hellenes to Veniselos the Cretan', first published in the *Manchester University Magazine* in January 1913. This strikingly illustrates the way in which Burrows, like so many of his phil-hellene contemporaries, was bowled over by the charismatic personality of the Greek statesman. The first and last verses run as follows:

> Veniselos! Veniselos!
> Do not fail us! Do not fail us!
> Now is come for thee the hour,
> To show forth thy master power.
> Lord of all Hellenic men,
> Make our country great again!

> Veniselos! Veniselos!
> Thou'lt not fail us! Thou'lt not fail us!
> Righteousness is on thy face;
> Strength thou hast to rule our race;
> Great in war and great in peace,
> Thou, our second Perikles![2]

While at the University of Manchester Burrows maintained good relations with the then important Greek community in the city and hoped that at some stage he might be able to persuade the Manchester Greeks to fund a lectureship in Modern Greek.

It was only when he moved to London in 1913 to take up the principalship of King's College that Burrows was able to give more concrete expression to his philhellenic sentiments. It should, however, be emphasised that while Burrows always had a very particular interest in, and emotional attachment to, Greece, under his principalship King's College became a powerhouse of academic propaganda in favour of national self-determination for the peoples of Eastern Europe. It was under Burrows' aegis that the School of Slavonic Studies (now, as the School of Slavonic and East European Studies, an independent institution of the University of London) was founded in 1915 as a part of the college. The most influential member of the staff of the newly founded School was R.W. Seton-Watson. Seton-Watson was an indefatigable champion of the oppressed of nationalities of the Habsburg Monarchy and was a co-founder, with Burrows and others, including H. Wickham Steed, the foreign editor of *The Times*, and A.F. Whyte, a Liberal MP, of the journal *The New Europe*. Between 1916 and 1920 *The New Europe* was influential in helping to shape British policy towards East and Central Europe, and Burrows was a frequent contributor.[3]

Burrows, by this time both an honorary doctor of the University of Athens and an honorary member of the Archaeological Society of Athens, was closely involved with another committed philhellene, William Pember Reeves, Director of the London School of Economics,[4] and two prominent Anglo-Greeks, D.J. Cassavetti and A.C. Ionides, in the foundation in 1913 of the Anglo-Hellenic League. The League had as its declared objectives, *inter alia*, the defence of the 'just claims and honour of Greece'; the removal of existing prejudices and the prevention of future misunderstandings between the 'British and Hellenic races' and also between the 'Hellenic and other races of South-Eastern Europe'. It also sought to spread information concerning Greece in Britain and to stimulate interest in Hellenic matters, together with the improvement of 'the social, educational, commercial and political relations of the two countries'. The offices of the League were situated in the Aldwych, convenient for both King's College and the London School of Economics, which are themselves in close proximity to each other. Virtually from its inception the League came to be identified with the projection of the aspirations of Venizelist Greece and this tendency became all the more pronounced when, on the outbreak of the First World War, the markedly Ententophil sympathies of Eleftherios Venizelos came into sharp conflict with the neutralist views of King Constantine. During the period between Venizelos' second forced resignation in 1915 and the formal recognition by the Entente Powers of Venizelos as Prime Minister of the whole of Greece in June 1917, the League acted as a vociferous instrument of Venizelist propaganda and argued strongly for the official recognition of the provisional government that Venizelos established in Salonica in the autumn of 1916. The League published numerous pamphlets of Anglo-Greek interest during this period, including a number of an explicitly political character, one of which, *The Crisis in Greece* (1915), was written by Burrows.

Throughout his principalship Burrows acted as tireless publicist on behalf of Venizelist Greece. He wrote numerous newspaper and periodical articles justifying Greece's territorial claims in general and Venizelos' policies in particular.[5] Some insight into the nature of Burrows' philhellenic thinking may be gleaned from this passage from an address that he gave to the Historical Association in 1919:

> There are points in common between Greece and Great Britain which exist between us and few of the people with whom we are allied. We are both a 'Nation of shopkeepers', and yet we have not been found wanting in the day of battle. We are both . . . a nation of sailors. At our best we turn out something of the same type of man.

Elsewhere in the same lecture he argued that 'the Greek race is not decadent, not on the down grade, but on the up grade – fertile, progressive, constantly expanding. It has at its head one of the great men of the century, a man who fulfils in his own person the ideals and aspirations of the race'.[6] He meant, of course, Venizelos.

It would appear that the idea of establishing a chair of Modern Greek in the University of London was first mooted at the time of the Balkan wars and that the initiative had come from British scholars, who presumably included Burrows. For D.J. Cassavetti, a member of a prominent Anglo-Greek family that had been established in Britain for some 80 years, writing towards the end of 1913, wrote that the institution of such a chair was 'one of the most practical suggestions that has been made for furthering the Hellenic cause' in Britain. An endowment of £10,000 would be the most required to secure the services of 'one of the most brilliant young Hellenists'. He hoped that Greeks and those of Greek origin settled in Britain would respond to British scholars who had expressed a desire to introduce the study of modern Greek among other modern languages at a great university.[7]

The earliest documentary evidence that has come to light of Burrows' involvement in the proposal to found a Modern Greek post at King's College is contained in a letter of 20 February 1915 that he received from A.M. Andreades, governor of the Bank of Greece and a distinguished economic historian. Andreades appears to have acted as the intermediary between Burrows and Venizelos for he wrote that the Greek Prime Minister had stated in a letter that he would be very pleased to grant £300 per year for the chair of 'Modern Greek History and Literature'. Venizelos had asked Andreades to approach a certain 'M' while passing through Rome on his way back to Greece from Paris. Andreades added that 'of course I shall speak to M on [sic] my own name and without mixing you in the least. This is to remain *strictly confidential* between us, as the details shall be settled and the money secured only when I shall reach Athens that is to say in a month. But as the question is settled in principle the details to be settled will be only of a formal nature'.[8]

Presumably Burrows and Venizelos had earlier been in contact about the possible establishment of such a chair and the decision to approach 'M' had been mutually agreed. The person cryptically referred to as 'M' was William Miller. Miller, an acute and sympathetic observer of the Greek scene, was a scholar journalist of independent means who had lived for many years in Athens but who was now based in the Italian capital.[9] It would appear that Burrows had already made provision for some teaching of Modern Greek at the college by this time, for there is a letter in the college archives from Nicolas Dioscorides, dated 19 February 1915, to the Principal asking for further information about the post, of whose establishment at the *Vasilikon Kollegion tou Londinou* he had recently read, of a teacher of Modern Greek.

Andreades' forecast that the matter would be settled within a matter of weeks was to prove highly optimistic, for by the time he had returned to Greece Venizelos had been forced to resign (in March 1915) by King Constantine I, who did not share the passionately pro-Entente views of his Prime Minister but rather believed that Greece's interests would best be served by neutrality in the conflict between the Entente and Central Powers. But Andreades was not discouraged by Venizelos' fall from office. In a letter of 22 May to Burrows he wrote it would be easy to get the subvention, if necessary, from the new Foreign Minister, Georgios Christakis Zografos, who was known for his pro-Entente views. Andreades believed it more practical, however, simply to await Venizelos' return to office, for he considered it out of the question that he would not return to power.[10] In elections held in the following month, June, Venizelos was indeed returned to power with a clear, although somewhat reduced, majority in Parliament. Because of the King's illness, however, he was not actually sworn in as Prime Minister until 23 August.

Shortly afterwards, on 16 September, Burrows wrote to Andreades that although he well understood that the Prime Minister would be overwhelmed with work at the present time he none the less hoped that Andreades might be able to raise the matter of the subvention with Venizelos. He believed it would be an 'extraordinarily appropriate and useful act' to make such a grant at this particular juncture: 'without in any way prejudicing political issues it would be a graceful act of practical sympathy, and if I were fortunate enough to secure Miller, it would have still further practical effects'. Burrows suggested that the Greek government should undertake to provide £300 a year 'for the funding of a Lectureship in Modern Greek Literature and History at University of London, King's College'. The advantage of such a wording was that it would leave the choice of the lecturer in the hands not of the university but of the college, 'which in the case in question would really be my hands'. Such a sum, moreover, would be enough to pay for a readership so that 'the College could easily secure the more dignified title if it felt satisfied that the man whom it wished to secure would be appointed'. Burrows added that he had already secured endowments for Italian and 'that the Belgrade government, though this is at present quite confidential, has already made us a grant for Serbian and South Slavonic'. He also had hopes of getting considerable endowments for Russian. 'It is extraordinarily important that Modern Greek should not be neglected and obscured.'

Andreades duly passed Burrows' letter on to Venizelos and on 30 September was in a position to reply that 'the premier thanks you most warmly for everything you are doing for Greece and congratulates you for doing so well your philhellenic work'. As for the chair of Modern Greek History and Literature, Venizelos had asked Andreades to write *at once* to say that in principle he was ready to make a grant of £300 and was now looking into ways of guaranteeing the payment for seven years. Andreades added that he had also written to Miller to secure his definite acceptance. When he had seen him in Rome the previous March he had been very inclined to accept, but had had some minor objections which he did not think it would be difficult to overcome, the chief of these being the possibility of his renewing his contract with the *Morning Post*. Andreades, however, had not pushed 'the thing too far', for on his reaching Athens Venizelos had been out of power.[11]

On 2 October Joannes Gennadius, the Greek minister in London, and himself a noted scholar and bibliophile,[12] wrote that he had been asked by Venizelos to inform Burrows that the Royal Government wished to guarantee for seven years *une chaire d'histoire et de littérature Grecques Modernes*. For this a special bill would need to be presented in parliament. Venizelos therefore wished to know urgently if there were any reason why the public should not know that a chair at King's College was officially subsidized by a foreign government. Two days later, on 4 October, Burrows informed Gennadius that he had consulted the authorities of the college and the Vice-Chancellor of the University of London, who wished to inform Venizelos that they were 'profoundly grateful to the Royal Government of Greece for the honour it has done us in offering to endow for seven years a Chair of Modern Greek History and Literature at King's College. The University and College Authorities will be proud to appoint to [a] Chair so endowed, and see no difficulty in the fact of its being publicly known what is the source of the endowment'. Burrows asked that Venizelos be informed of the intense pleasure that he personally felt 'as an ardent Phil-Hellene' that it should fall to him as Principal of the college 'to be the medium of receiving this gift from Greece to England at such a crisis in the history of our two nations'.[13]

This particular initiative, however, was thwarted by the fact that shortly after Burrows wrote to Gennadius, Venizelos, on 7 October, was forced by King Constantine to resign for the second time. Following the Bulgarian mobilization in the wake of the secret treaty between King Ferdinand of Bulgaria and the Central Powers, Venizelos and his supporters had argued that Greece, under the terms of the Greek–Serbian treaty of 1913, was obliged to go to the assistance of Serbia, the principal target of the Bulgarian mobilization. His opponents had argued that the obligation lapsed in the case of the involvement of a non-Balkan power, namely Austria-Hungary. King Constantine agreed to Venizelos' request for the mobilization of the armed forces but was still determined to maintain Greek neutrality and hence demanded Venizelos' resignation. Venizelos' replacement as Prime Minister by Alexandros Zaimis was to mark the beginning of what is known as the 'National Schism', the division of Greece into two violently antagonistic, and at times warring, camps: the Venizelists and the supporters of King Constantine. Venizelos himself withdrew from active participation in the political process and called for a boycott of the December 1915 elections. In October 1916, following a coup in the city by Venizelist officers, Venizelos created a provisional government in Salonica. At first the Entente Powers withheld recognition from the Salonica government but this attitude changed following an armed clash between British and French troops and the royalist government in Athens in December 1916. Relations between the Entente Powers and the Athens government continued to deteriorate even further and culminated in the ousting of King Constantine in June 1917 in favour of his second son Alexander. Venizelos now became Prime Minister of a united Greece and forthwith committed Greek troops to the Salonica front, which had been established by the Entente Allies in the autumn of 1915.

During the period that Venizelos was out of office Burrows was naturally forced, for the time being at least, to drop the idea of funding the new post with a subvention from the Greek government. The apparent triumph of the anti-Venizelists in Greece in the autumn of 1915, however, made Burrows more determined than ever to proceed with a project which now became even more closely associated in his mind with the promotion of the Venizelist cause. The establishment of the chair was one of the principal means by which Burrows sought to further the interests of his idol Venizelos. Moreover, Burrows' philhellenism at this time did not find expression in mere rhetoric alone. In October 1915 when Serbia was gravely threatened after Bulgaria had thrown in its lot with the Central Powers, Burrows managed to induce the British government to adopt a policy of offering the *enosis* of Cyprus with Greece in return for Greece's entry into the war on the side of Serbia. The plan, which Burrows formulated in concert with R.W. Seton-Watson, went as follows. The governor of Cyprus was to be instructed to inform the Archbishop and the Greek members of the Legislative Council that Britain was ready to cede Cyprus to Greece at once, and also to guarantee for ten years the territories which Greece had won by the Treaty of Bucharest, on the one condition that Greece should enter the war on the side of the Entente. The governor was instructed to allow the Archbishop to proceed forthwith to Athens to appeal to King Constantine and the Greek Parliament to accept the offer, which would never be repeated. At the same time the British minister in Athens, Sir Francis Elliot, was to be instructed to inform Venizelos of the offer and to ensure that it was heavily publicized in the Venizelist press in an effort to put pressure on the government to accept. Burrows' plan was adopted more or less *in toto* by the British government. The governor of Cyprus at the time, Sir John Clauson, was, however, less than enthusiastic and spoke of the awkwardness of having to inform the 'Loyal Moslem', i.e. Turkish, minority. Moreover, the proposal foundered when Sir Edward Grey, the British Foreign Secretary, failed to prosecute it with sufficient vigour. The failure to exploit the pressure of Venizelist public opinion enabled the Greek cabinet to turn down the offer. Thus what was perhaps the most opportune chance of bringing about the *enosis* of Cyprus and Greece was lost.[14]

Burrows was naturally bitterly disappointed by this setback, but his enthusiasm for the Venizelist cause if anything increased in fervour. So closely identified, indeed, did he become with Venizelism that in November 1916, shortly after Venizelos had established his provisional government in Salonica, the Greek statesman, in a long letter to Burrows, outlined the situation in Greece and asked him to act as the 'semi-official representative' of the Provisional Government in London for as long as it was not officially recognised by the British government. He enclosed with his letter to Burrows a letter for Sir Edward Grey, asking him to accept Burrows in this capacity: *L'éminent Professeur Burrows, du King's College, qui, suivant les libérales traditions de sa noble et grande Nation, n'a cessé de donner à l'Hellénisme les témoignages de la plus inestimable amitié, veut bien se charger d'être à Londres le représentant officieux du Gouvernement Provisoire.*[15] The matter was not pursued, however, for soon afterwards Gennadius was to resign as the minister of the government of King Constantine in London and he was thus able to act as the official representative of the Venizelist Government of National Defence in Britain.[16] Burrows' activities did not go wholly unchallenged, as the publication in late 1917 of a pamphlet entitled *Pseudo-Philhellenes: a letter to E. Venizelos on the duplicity of Principal Burrows of King's College*, indicates.

The establishment of a post in Modern Greek at King's clearly, in Burrows' mind, formed part and parcel of the propaganda effort being waged on behalf of Venizelist Greece. Burrows was determined to press on with the project despite Venizelos' fall from office. Pending the establishment of such a post, in the autumn of 1915, and apparently using the college's own resources, Burrows made modest provision for the teaching of Modern Greek at the college. On 11 October, Mary Gardner, the author of a tract on Modern Greek,[17] wrote to Burrows that she would be happy to teach Greek conversation to some nurses who were apparently about to be dispatched to the Salonica front, and was duly appointed as lecturer in Modern Greek, a post in which she was succeeded by Christos Kessary in 1917. She added that '... you can't think how it *hurts* not to have Greece rushing to our help. What would poor old George Gordon Noel Byron have thought of their present *official* attitude?' A few days later she vouchsafed the view that Constantine 'is being like Canute and does not know when the tide is coming in'.

In order to put Modern Greek studies in the college on a sounder footing Burrows, now that the prospect of Greek government funding had receded, began increasingly to look to the well-established, prosperous and largely Venizelist Greek community in Britain as a source of funds.[19] It appears, too, that he was now thinking in terms of establishing a chair rather than a lectureship or readership. That Burrows was able to assure potential donors that the proposal enjoyed the personal support of Venizelos was clearly a powerful asset, as the following letter of 23 May 1916 from D. Theophilatus, a Greek established in the City of London, indicates: 'Mr Venizelos' interest in this scheme is quite evident and I feel proud, as one of his followers, to see that he grasped so cleverly the importance of this scheme .... Now, unfortunately, that he is not in power, we, the Greeks in London, must feel happy that we have the opportunity of helping the scheme'.[20] At one stage Burrows believed that it might be possible to raise the entire endowment from a single source, Miss Helena Schilizzi, a member of a rich and well-established Anglo-Greek family who was subsequently to marry Eleftherios Venizelos. In July 1916, following an evening at the Cassavettis[21] during which Mr and Miss Kephala had outlined Miss Schilizzi's and Mr Embiricos' interest in promoting the activities of the Anglo-Hellenic League, Burrows wrote to Miss Schilizzi to suggest how her ideas as to the promotion of the Greek cause in England might best be furthered by the endowment of a chair in Modern Greek literature and history.

The only way of carrying out Miss Schilizzi's ideas, with which he had every sympathy, Burrows wrote, was by attracting to London 'an English Phil-Hellene of high standing who should have his whole time to devote to the cause of Greece'. He agreed with her that 'where we are weak is on the English side, and above all that we have not yet tapped the great potential force of the English public school and University man who has been brought up on Ancient Greek literature'. No paid secretary of the Anglo-Hellenic League of the ordinary kind could achieve much in this direction as he could only carry out orders. What was needed was 'a directing force that has time to think out orders'. Neither Pember Reeves, Director of the London School of Economics and a leading light in the Anglo-Hellenic League, nor Burrows himself, with their huge administrative burdens, would have the time 'to carry through things on the ideally large scale'. Someone of the standing and energy of William Miller was needed and Burrows understood from Miss Effie Kephala[22] that Miss Schilizzi had herself mentioned Miller in this connection. The only possible way of bringing Miller back from Rome and of giving him the permanent position 'which would enable him to do what you want' would be by the foundation of a professorship of 'Modern Greek Literature and History' at the University of London and that 'we should secure his election to it'. 'We could not guarantee that election, but I think that there is little doubt that we could secure it'. A professorship at £600 p.a. would be more likely to secure Miller than a readership at £300, and an endowment bringing in interest would be preferable to a guarantee of income over a number of years. Burrows concluded by emphasizing that 'Mr Miller would have very little routine work, and would be able to give practically his full time to the general promotion of the cause'.

D.J. Cassavetti forwarded Burrows' letter to Miss Schilizzi on 14 July, with a covering note of his own. Cassavetti wrote that Dr Burrows felt very strongly that the 'best way of obtaining a "whole time" man of ability and position to run the Greek cause in England by means of the [Anglo-Hellenic] League' was through the establishment of a chair at London University. Cassavetti had initially been doubtful, but Burrows had explained that the incumbent of the chair 'would really have very little of his time taken up with the University duties, and would have the bulk of his time available to act as an unpaid official of the League'. This would put him in a much stronger position with the public than a paid secretary who could in any case, if necessary, be hired later.[23] On the same day, 14 July, Cassavetti informed Burrows that he had heard from Miss Schilizzi that she would very likely find herself all the funds needed for the professorship: 'so this looks very hopeful'.[24] On the strength of these promising indications, Burrows wrote to J.L. Hartog, the Academic Registrar of the University, on 17 July to say that he hoped soon to bring off the establishment of the chair: 'the donor will probably want the title of the Chair to be Modern Greek History and Literature, possibly adding the word "and Byzantine"'. 'The Classics

Board,' he added, 'the Mediaeval and Modern Languages Board, and the History Board would all seem to have claims to appointment.' Miller, he believed, would be an ideal candidate and he suggested as external experts the classicists Gilbert Murray or Sir J.E. Sandys, the Byzantinist J.B. Bury and Gennadius. Hartog replied the following day that he believed that only the Mediaeval and Modern Languages Board need be involved.[25]

Two months later Burrows wrote to William Miller in Rome to ask whether he would be willing to be a candidate for the chair, although no certain copy of this approach appears to survive. An undated and incomplete draft of a letter to Miller in the archives of King's College may date from this period. In this Burrows assured Miller that he would be at the 'heart of things, and would have unlimited opportunities for journalistic work whether in the *New Europe* or in any older established magazines, and equal opportunity for public lectures on propagandist subjects in our Great Hall at King's'.[26] If Miller was willing to stand then he was requested to send a *cursus vitae*. Burrows was also anxious to know whether it would make any difference to his answer if the post were to be advertised and, in particular, whether he would only stand if an invitation were addressed to him without advertisement. 'This is a matter which some people find important, and our procedure need not be rigid in the matter.'

In his reply of 19 September Miller wrote that he had one preliminary question, namely the source of the funds for the endowment of the proposed chair. 'If they are to be provided directly or indirectly by a foreign government, then I may at once decline all further consideration of the matter.' It was for this reason that he had been unable to entertain the former scheme. This was presumably a reference to the approach from Venizelos via Andreades early in 1915 when it was proposed that the Greek government should put up £300 p.a. for a period of seven years. 'Such an arrangement would completely sap the independence of the professor or reader, would expose him to just criticism, and would quite nullify all his efforts, however honest, to advocate the cause which he had at heart.' In his experience as a journalist he had seen several such cases and nothing would induce him to put himself 'directly or indirectly in such a position'. If, however, the funds were to be subscribed by British subscribers that would be another matter. Miller asked to be enlightened confidentially on that point. As he had private means and no dependents, salary was not of primary importance. On 25 September Burrows replied to Miller that he had not yet secured the funds but that he thought that he most probably could obtain them if he had a fair chance of getting Miller to accept the post. He could assure Miller that the money for the chair would come from individuals, principally Anglo-Greeks, 'not an obscurantist or bigoted body', and not from the Greek government. But he did not quite agree that if such foreign government funds were given 'to a public body which has a free election, and not to an individual, they would in any way hamper the individual's independence'. The college had not, for instance, felt any reluctance in receiving a small sum from the Serbian government. To this letter Miller replied on 5 October that, for financial and other reasons, he preferred not to commit himself until the war was over.[27]

The reasons for the failure of Miss Schilizzi to provide the entire endowment, as Burrows and Cassavetti had hoped, are unclear, although she was
to make one of the largest individual donations. Burrows now realized that
he would have to appeal to the Greek community in Britain at large. It was in
this connection that he was in close touch with Nicholas Eumorfopoulos, a
member of a prominent Anglo-Greek family who taught physics at University College, London. A fellow of the college since 1900, Eumorfopoulos,
popularly known as 'Eumo', took an active part in college life over a period
of more than 50 years. Eumorfopoulos, in turn, was in contact with a
number of influential members of the Greek community. On 1 March 1917,
for instance, he wrote to M.A. Mitaranga, a wealthy Greek based in
Marseilles, that while confidentially Burrows had his eye on Miller it was
none the less most important that his name should not in any way get into
print. Eumorfopoulos regarded it as important that the professor should
be an Englishman 'as his opinion would carry weight when lecturing or
writing to the papers'. He added that it was certainly 'rather humiliating that
no Modern Greek Chair exists: most people think that there is practically no
connection with Ancient Greek. It is necessary to show that there is a
continuous tradition'.[28] A few days later, in a long letter of 7 March 1917,
Burrows himself wrote to M.A. Mitaranga. He expressed his pleasure that
various prominent members of the Greek community had taken up the
project of founding and endowing 'a department of Modern Greek and
Byzantine literature, history and philology' at King's College and proceeded
to outline his views on the importance of such a chair and to discuss some of
the practicalities associated with such an endowment:

> The importance to the Greek Nation as a whole of the establishment of
> such a department, in the centre of the British Empire, can scarcely be
> exaggerated. The permanence of the classical Greek tradition in the
> education of the upper and middle classes ought to make it possible
> and natural for Modern Greek to have a unique hold on the interest
> and affection of the English governing classes. Unfortunately there is a
> wide gulf fixed between Ancient and Modern Greek literature and
> history, and the average educated Englishman sees no connection
> between the two. This will continue to be the case so long as the
> professors and teachers of Ancient Greek can be counted by the score,
> and occupy the most important positions in all the universities of the
> kingdom, while the teachers of Modern Greek, where they exist at all,
> are untrained journalists, or language masters without salary, standing
> or dignity.[29] It is not sufficiently realised among Greeks in England or
> in the Mother-country, that education in Ancient Greek literature and
> history is immeasurably deeper and wider-spread in England than in
> France or in any other country in Europe, and that public opinion in
> parliament and the press depends practically entirely on the opinion of
> the classes so educated.
>
> The opportunity, therefore, is unique. It is not a matter of sentiment
> nor an academic fad. It is a vital, practical matter affecting the political
> and business interests of the kingdom of Greece, and the whole of the

Greek race. It would be difficult to find any object on which expenditure would be a sounder national investment.

The capital sum necessary would be between £16,000 and £20,000 (the final sum raised appears to have been nearer the lower figure) which should preferably be in the form of an endowment rather than a guaranteed income for a given number of years. Burrows was clearly sensitive to the possibility that the donors might wish to exercise some sort of control over the chair for he went out of his way to stress that the university was obliged by statute to make all appointments itself, 'not only a necessary point ... but ... a highly commendable one' if the chair were to attract 'the highest type of man who alone would do justice to the dignity of a great subject'. At the same time he believed that the appointments procedure would ensure 'that the wishes of the donors should be impartially carried into effect'. The Senate could only appoint a professor on the advice of a Board of Advisors, whose advice had never yet been rejected. This board would consist of the Vice-Chancellor and Principal of the University, the Principal of King's College, three members of the Professorial Board of the College, 'who could be made thoroughly acquainted with the wishes of the donors', and three external experts who would be chosen *ad hoc* for their knowledge of the field, and who would have to resign if they became candidates. Even if it were legally possible, which it was not, to include a representative of the donors among the electors,[30] difficulties would inevitably arise in future years as the surviving donors became fewer and fewer. 'From the point of view of the highest Greek national interest, it is far safer to trust that the right external experts will be chosen by the knowledge and good feeling of a permanent and impartial body like the University.' This had been the view taken by the powerful outside committee that had collected funds for the Cervantes Chair of Spanish at King's College. In the event Joannes Gennadius, the chairman of the Subscribers' Committee, was included in the Board of Advisors which made the first appointment to the chair.

Burrows advised that the trust deed should state that the purposes of the new Department were 'Modern Greek and Byzantine literature, history and philology' and that discretion be given to the Board of Advisors on each occasion that the chair was advertised to make an appointment in either the philological or historical side according to the strength of the field 'and other general considerations'. Thus if William Miller were a candidate then the appointment should be in history and literature, but were a great philologist such as Professor N.G. Politis to apply then the appointment could be in philology. It would, Burrows added, be quite in order for appointments in the department to be restricted to those of either British or Greek nationality. Both on the British and Greek sides there seems to have been some fear that a German (or Turkish) scholar might apply and a belief that such a provision would exclude such a potential embarrassment.

Burrows next turned to the question of the endowment. It might be suggested that the money be retained permanently under the control of the trustees and that appointments be made for a term of years. Burrows argued that there were three objections to such a course. Firstly, the trustees would not be able to influence the selection as the university was bound by statute to adhere to the selection procedure he had outlined above. Secondly, since the university would be responsible for the professor's salary, it would be likely to insist on appointing one or more of the trustees. Lastly, and most important, no Englishman of standing ('and in many cases an Englishman would be the best appointment from the Greek point of view') would accept a position 'which even seemed to put him in the pay of a body which could be represented as remotely connected with a foreign government'. Burrows then went on to quote from Miller's letter to him of 19 September 1916. Burrows added that he felt that someone of the stature of Miller would raise the same objections if the Greek community in London could remove him from his chair after a certain number of years. On the other hand he thought that it would be possible for the trustees to retain control of the capital sum, while allowing the university complete discretion over the income, until the professor resigned, reached the retiring age of 65 or died. In any of these eventualities the whole matter could be reconsidered.[31]

Burrows' letter was now circulated among potential subscribers by Mitaranga, while Burrows himself pursued Sir Basil Zaharoff, the enigmatic and enormously wealthy arms magnate, who had already offered £25,000 to endow a Chair of Aviation at Imperial College of the University of London.[32] On 19 June 1917 he wrote to the MP and publicist T.P. O'Connor, who described himself as 'one of the oldest survivors of the Philhellenes of the days of Gladstone',[33] to say that Zaharoff had expressed interest in the scheme and asking him to back it up with all his persuasiveness. '... If Mr Zaharoff is like most rich men, he wishes no more than the rest of us to do all the giving himself. If he really means that he does not want the chair to be called after his name, probably the most effective and economical scheme would be if he were to give £10,000 on the condition that another £10,000 were collected elsewhere ...' On 3 October Mitaranga wrote to Burrows to alert him to the fact that Zaharoff, now recovered from a very serious illness, was currently visiting London. He enclosed Zaharoff's visiting card and suggested that he see him, preferably accompanied by T.P. O'Connor. Such a meeting appears to have taken place in the drawing room of the Principal's residence at the college, for on 29 December Burrows wrote to Zaharoff to remind him that, although he had said that he could not give as much to the appeal as he might have done in other circumstances, 'you would not altogether refuse me'. He pointed out that Venizelos, during his recent visit to London, in the course of which he had been rapturously received at a meeting in the Mansion House,[34] had assigned to the appeal fund £2,000 which had been given him by Sir Lucas Ralli, a director of Ralli Brothers. On the other hand one or two subscribers had not given as much as Mitaranga had hoped, while a certain Mr Pandeli had 'completely repudiated the £1,000 he promised'.[35] This was the kind of very shocking behaviour, as Burrows wrote to Mitaranga on 28 January 1918, that 'not only does this particular scheme harm but damages the national reputation'. He wondered whether something might be done to instil a sense of shame in Pandeli. One suggestion made by Burrows was that Pandeli should be told that his subscription had been notified to Venizelos, who had himself subscribed on the understanding that only a certain amount more needed to be raised.[36] It appears that in the end Zaharoff, despite expressions of goodwill, was not among the subscribers to the chair.

At some stage during 1917 a committee of subscribers, initially known as the Koraes Chair of Modern Greek Fund, was established, with Nicholas Eumorfopoulos being appointed secretary. Eumorfopoulos, like Burrows, took advantage of the enthusiasm created by Venizelos' visit to London to circularize in December 1917 potential donors, enclosing Burrows' letter to Mitaranga of 7 March 1917 with a covering letter of his own. Eumorfopoulos noted that, at a meeting organized by the Greek *paroikia* of London, Venizelos had stated that 'we in Greece are proud of the Greek Communities in England, and in return we would ask two things of these Communities: that they also should be proud of Greece and that they should not allow the Greek language to be forgotten'. The establishment of the chair, so Eumorfopoulos argued, would help to secure both objects: 'it will show both to us and the British People the continuity of Greek Civilization and the Greek Language and will teach these lessons in the very centre of the Empire'. During his recent visit to London Venizelos had expressed his 'ardent desire' that the chair should be founded without delay. The fact that the Greek government had voted an annual subsidy of 7,500 drachmas (approximately £300) considerably diminished the amount which it was absolutely necessary to collect, although it was 'very advisable to be as independent as possible from Government endowment'. He pointed out that chairs had been, or were being, established in the university 'in Serbian, Portuguese,[37] Spanish and the Scandinavian languages'. 'If, therefore, this Chair is not founded, Modern Greek will be the only language unrepresented. I need hardly say that this must not take place'.[38]

The bill to grant a subsidy for the Koraes Chair was given its first and second readings in the Greek Parliament on 7 and 9 (OS) October and received the royal assent on 18 November (OS). The one clause bill (1064/1917) gave authority to the Ministry of Religious Affairs and Public Education to make an annual grant of 7,500 drachmas for a period of seven years for the 'Chair of Modern Greek History and Literature' established at King's College of the University of London.[39] After Burrows had been formally notified early in December by Gennadius that the bill had been passed in the Greek Parliament, a committee, consisting of the chairman of the Delegacy (the governing body of the college), Viscount Hambledon, the treasurer, the Hon. R.C. Parsons, and the Principal, together with three representatives of the Professorial Board, was set up by the college to confer with the subscribers as to the conditions of the appointment and the scope of the new department. In a letter circulated to members of this committee on 3 January 1918 Burrows envisaged that the only matter likely to raise difficulty was that the subscribers would probably not wish to hand over the capital endowment but would rather seek to appoint their own trustees, with wide-ranging powers of investment, to hold it, while guaranteeing to the university £600 per year for the period of the first tenure of the chair.[40] The reason for this proposed stipulation was that the donors believed that they would be so able to invest the capital of the fund as to ensure that the purchasing power of the accruing income could be maintained.[41] Such a provision was included in the draft deed of gift, dated January 1918. Clause three to the effect that lectures might be given under the terms of the Koraes endowment at other colleges of the university and on subjects other than those mentioned in the title of the chair was apparently included so that it might be possible for lectures on the Greek economy to be given by agreement at the London School of Economics.

Burrows was correct in his surmise that the university's major objection to the draft deed of gift concerned the trustees' wish to retain control over the capital of the fund. On 28 February Burrows wrote to Viscount Hambledon, the chairman of the Delegacy, to assure him that while the draft trust deed contained no absolute guarantee that the professor's salary would always be forthcoming, Burrows was confident that it would be, given that the three proposed trustees were the London, County and Westminster Bank, M. Embiricos, an 'extremely rich ship owner', and G. Eumorfopoulos, a director of Ralli Brothers and the elder brother of Nicholas Eumorfopoulos, the honorary secretary of the Subscribers' Committee. Sir Lucas Ralli had bowed out of being a trustee on the grounds of age. Both Embiricos and Eumorfopoulos were men of substance and the college, moreover, would be kept in touch with the Greek community under clause four, section two. Although Burrows thought it unlikely that 'another government in Greece would be so willing to offend England as to withdraw an annual grant once made',[42] he believed that it would be prudent to pay the salary of the permanent professor out of the English trustee fund, while it was probable that an Englishman would prefer if possible not to be paid out of a grant from a foreign government. On the other hand he thought that it would be unwise to be too specific on this question in dealings with the Greek authorities and preferable to treat the £600 provided by the trustees and the £300 by the Greek government as a joint sum out of which both the professor and lecturer were to be appointed. Otherwise the Greek government might regard it as somewhat *infra dig* if it was seen to be providing only for the lectureship and not for the chair.[43]

Hambledon replied to Burrows on 2 March that, while no expert, he was worried about a possible conflict of opinion arising between the trustees and the college out of clauses five and six as to who was to determine that the intention of the trust could not be carried out. On the same day Clifford Edgar wrote to Burrows that he was worried by the 'very unusual powers of investment' and the absence of any provision for the eventual handing over of the endowment. He, too, found clause six the most open to question, regarding it as quite unacceptable if, whatever liability the university might be under at the time, it left the trustees free to divert the capital to other uses 'merely by declaring their "opinion" that it was no longer expedient to employ the Endowment Fund in promoting the original studies'. On 3 March, Sir Edward Busk, the university's legal adviser, wrote to the Principal of the University, Sir Edwin Cooper Perry, to state that he could not advise the Senate to inaugurate the department on the proposed terms for a number of reasons. He had doubts as to how the payment of the professor's salary could be enforced under the proposed deed to which 'the University is not even made a party' and also about the wide discretion granted to the trustees to invest 'in anything anywhere'. He strongly advised that the endowment fund be transferred 'to the University as a Corporation'. If the university were to appoint a professor, then it must be for life or for a fixed term of years at least.[44]

The matter was further discussed at a meeting of the Subscribers' Committee held at the college on 5 March 1918, attended by Gennadius, four subscribers, including Nicholas Eumorfopoulos, Burrows and a representative of the London, County and Westminster Bank. At this meeting Gennadius, as chairman, declared his opposition to the large powers of investment given to the trustees. Moreover, he thought it more consonant with the dignity of the Greek community to hand over the capital to the university.[45] The other subscribers present apparently concurred. Presumably this decision was communicated to the eight representatives of the university and college who subsequently attended the meeting to thank the subscribers for their generosity in setting up the chair. This larger meeting was apparently attended by the Vice-Chancellor himself, who had earlier expressed to Burrows a wish to be present, although not as vice-chancellor if he were expected to give his assent to financial proposals that had yet to be placed formally before the Finance Committee of the Senate.

> The oral examination of a donated horse is always unpleasant, but it has to be done, and the subscribers ought to make it clear that the University accepts no risks in taking the gift, even though they are allowed to make ducks and drakes with the capital.[46]

A few days later, on 11 March, Burrows wrote to A.C. Ionides, a member of the Subscribers' Committee, that the university authorities were 'intensely relieved' that Gennadius and the four other subscribers present at the meeting had been in favour of handing the endowment over to the university.[47] It appears, however, that Ionides, who had not been present at the meeting, still objected to handing over the capital and was considering withdrawing his own contribution. This possibility alarmed Burrows, who feared that if word reached Miller of any difference of opinion between the university and the subscribers, he would be certain not to accept the chair. He was also worried that disagreement on the issue between the subscribers at this stage did not augur well for their future unanimity if they were to retain control over the capital: '... Forgive me for saying,' he wrote somewhat peevishly, 'that the very fact which Eumorfopoulos and you insist on, that Anglo-Greeks will not act together on committee, and which you singularly justified by not turning up on Tuesday yourself, though the eight University representatives, all of them far busier men, did turn up, casts in itself some doubt on the trustee deed.'[48]

It was not until April of 1918 that a compromise was formally reached between the trustees and the university authorities over control of the endowment. By this the subscribers undertook to offer such capital sums invested in trustee stock as would bring in a yearly income of not less than £600 per annum. The university was empowered, during the tenure of the professorship, to alter the investments within the limits of British trust law. Up to £600 per annum could be applied to the professor's salary, any surplus being devoted to the departmental library, to the funding of scholarships, to the provision of lectureships in Greek economics or other academic subjects related to Greece either in King's College or in other institutions of the university. The subscribers expressed the wish to be sent the scheme of work to be undertaken by the department before the beginning of each session, and requested that every three years a report on the work actually carried out by the department should be sent to the Subscribers' Committee with a request for criticisms and suggestions. At the same time the subscribers reserved the right to review the conditions attaching to the chair whenever there was a vacancy arising out of resignation, retirement or death, and, on such a vacancy, to have the power to withdraw the entire endowment if they thought it desirable. Any such decision to terminate the endowment would have to be taken by no fewer than eight of the twelve members of the Subscribers' Committee.[49] On 24 April Eumorfopoulos sent Burrows a list of those who, subject to their agreement, were to become members of the Subscribers' Committee: M. Embiricos, G. Eumorfopoulos and G. Marchetti were to act as joint treasurers and Nicholas Eumorfopoulos was to act as secretary. The London community was to be represented by Gennadius, A.C. Ionides and Helena Schilizzi; the Liverpool community by Alexander Pallis; the Manchester community by C.C. Demetriadi and G.B. Zochonis; and the Marseilles community by J.N. Metaxa and M.A. Mitaranga. It was subsequently resolved that three members of the Subscribers' Committee would constitute a quorum, while a resolution signed by all members of the committee was to be as valid as if passed at a meeting of the committee.[50]

At the same time the Subscribers' Committee decided to drop its previous insistence that the holder of the chair be of either British or Greek nationality, partly because of the difficulty in reaching a satisfactory definition of nationality. Eumorfopoulos declared that the committee were prepared to leave it 'to the good sense of the University not to appoint a Turk'. Burrows had told Eumorfopoulos that the original purpose of the nationality stipulations had been to prevent the election of 'a Bulgarian Greek'.[51] It had originally been provided that any holder of a teaching post in the department should be 'either a British subject whose father was at his birth a British subject or a Greek subject or of Greek nationality although a Turkish subject or the subject of any other state'. The difficulties in defining nationality among a people of the *diaspora* such as the Greeks pre-eminently were, and are, had led the subscribers to provide for a waiver of this condition in the case of candidates whom they considered 'to be of British or Greek descent in the popular sense and whose national sympathies they are satisfied are British or Greek'.[52]

On 26 April Burrows sent copies of the new scheme, with its provision for the handing over of the endowment for the period of the first tenure of the chair only, to, among others, Sir Cooper Perry and Sir Edward Busk. Burrows said that he would have been happier if this condition had been dispensed with but it was the result of a compromise without which important subscriptions might have been withdrawn.[53] In any case he was hopeful that, as the consent of two thirds of the Subscribers' Committee was necessary for any change in the conditions attaching to the endowment, in practice its permanence would not be affected. Busk replied on 28 April that the new scheme was an 'immense improvement' from the university's point of view. He asked Burrows to confirm to him that if, on a vacancy, the Subscribers' Committee did vote for a change in the conditions attaching to the chair, then it would be open to the university either to comply or to give it up. This Burrows was able to do after corresponding with Eumorfopoulos.[54]

The Academic Council of the University, and subsequently the Senate, were now able to give their blessing to the foundation of the chair. The Senate recommended that the chair be established, with effect from October 1918, unless a postponement was necessitated by the war. The full title of the holder of the chair was to be the 'Koraes Professor of Modern Greek', although the chair subsequently became known as the Koraes Chair of Modern Greek and Byzantine History, Language and Literature. No evidence appears to survive as to why the chair was named after Adamantios Korais (1748–1833), the great classical scholar and intellectual mentor of the movement for Greek independence. The choice was made, however, presumably because Korais, despite the fact that there is no evidence that he ever visited the island, was a fanatical Chiot patriot and many of the subscribers were themselves of Chiot origin. Consideration was, in the early stages, given to calling the chair after Venizelos, although Burrows believed that this would have been a tactical mistake, while Eumorfopoulos, in principle, rather objected to naming it after a living person.[55] Tenure was to be for five years in the first instance, with the professor being eligible for re-appointment up to the retiring age of 65. The Board of Advisors were, however, empowered, if they saw fit, to appoint to retiring age on the occasion of the first appointment. The professor would be required to take general direction of the Department of Modern Greek and Byzantine History, Language and Literature at King's College, which was to offer instruction in the day and, if necessary, in the evening.

The Board of Advisors for the Chair was to be constituted as follows. The Vice-Chancellor, the Principal Officer of the University, and the Principal of King's College were to be *ex-officio* members. Professor J.B. Bury, the historian of the later Roman Empire (with Professor C.W.C. Oman as substitute), Sir F.C. Kenyon, the director of the British Museum (with Dr W.C. Leaf as substitute) and His Excellency Dr J. Gennadius, the Greek minister (with R.M. Dawkins as substitute), were to constitute the external experts. The Board was to be completed by the three nominees of the Professorial Board at King's College, F.J.C. Hearnshaw, Professor of History, R.W. Seton-Watson, and W.C.F. Walters, Professor of Classics.[56] The appointment of Gennadius, the chairman of the Subscribers' Committee, as one of the external experts advising on the appointment resulted from lobbying on Burrows' part. As early as the summer of 1916, when Burrows had high hopes that Miss Helena Schilizzi would provide the entire endowment, he had written to P.L. Hartog, the Academic Registrar of the University, to suggest as external experts the hellenists Sir Gilbert Murray or Sir J.E. Sandys, J.B. Bury and Gennadius.[57] Again in January 1917 Burrows had written to the Chairman of the Board of Studies in Classics, to which the new chair had been assigned, strongly to support the appointment of Gennadius as an external expert. He held honorary doctorates from both Oxford and Cambridge and had done 'quite a lot of good scholarly work'. There was, moreover, the precedent of the Spanish ambassador who had been appointed one of the external experts for the Cervantes Chair at King's college.[58]

On 22 May M.J.M. Hill, the Chairman of the Academic Council, wrote to Eumorfopoulos to express the grateful thanks of the Senate for the endowment. A few days earlier the Vice-Chancellor, Sir Cooper Perry, asked Gennadius to convey the university's thanks for the annual subvention of 7,500 drachmas to the Greek government and assured him of the 'great gratification that is felt by the Senate of the University of London at the splendid opportunity that is thus given to the citizens of London for acquiring a knowledge of the History, Literature, and Language of the Greek people. It will be a bond that will unite still more closely the two allied nations'.[59] Now that the endowment had been formally accepted by the university, Burrows moved promptly to publicize the new foundation through an article which he wrote for *The Times* of 16 May 1918, and which, at his request, appeared anonymously. In what appears to be a draft of this article Burrows optimistically declared that Greece had shaken free from 'the party strife in which the intrigues of the late [sic] King had so long involved her' and was now an ally of the Entente. He hailed Venizelos as the founder of the department, pointing to the fact that one of his last acts before being forced to resign as Prime Minister in October 1915 had been to cable Burrows that he wished to vote a subsidy for the chair in the Greek Parliament and that one of his first acts on returning to power in 1917 had been to revive this earlier proposal.[60]

Part of the article duly appeared in *The Times* on 16 May, together with an advertisement listing the subscribers to date and stating that further subscriptions were still welcome.[61] A similar article was published on the same day in *The Manchester Guardian*. The *Times* article, however, had appeared in a truncated form and on 17 May Burrows wrote to the editor to complain that not only had the article been severely abridged, despite assurances to the contrary given by H. Wickham-Steed, the foreign editor, but it had not been prominently displayed. He had asked for reprints of the article and the advertisement to be made for sending to Athens but the article had been so shortened as to be of no use for this purpose. He conceded that urgent news might perhaps have justified cutting the article but on the 16th there had been 'a complete absence of any sort of interesting news', while page five, where the article had appeared, had contained paragraph after paragraph 'which could well have been postponed or altogether omitted without great loss', a view in which he was sure that educated opinion would be on his side. He realised that the editorial and advertising departments of *The Times* should be kept distinct but it was none the less 'right and natural' that in a case like the present 'where the motive is beyond suspicion, the concurrent insertion of a long and expensive advertisement should induce consideration for an accompanying paragraph, when both are obviously meant for most useful propaganda and reprints of both have been ordered'. Not surprisingly Burrows received a sharp rebuff from the editor's secretary, J. Webb, who, on 20 May, wrote that the editor had been astonished that Burrows should commit himself to the statement that the item about the Modern Greek chair was the only interesting news in the paper. The suggestion that the insertion of the advertisement should induce consideration for the article on the chair was quite inadmissible. The appearance, form and position of the article was entirely a matter for the discretion of the editor, who did not expect 'to be lectured', in the tone of your letter, on the right conduct of his business'.[62]

NOTES

1. George Glasgow, *Ronald Burrows: A Memoir* (London, 1924), p. 30.
2. Reprinted in ibid., pp. 161–2.
3. See Hugh and Christopher Seton-Watson, *The Making of a New Europe: R.W. Seton-Watson and the Last Years of Austria-Hungary* (London, 1981) and H. Hanak, 'The New Europe, 1916–1920', *The Slavonic and East European Review*, xxix (1961), pp. 369–99.
4. Pember Reeves' biographer records that he 'never tired of ... drawing parallels between ancient Greece and modern New Zealand'. Like Burrows he did 'most utterly and completely trust' Venizelos and he, too, was something of a poetaster, being the author of 'Greek Fire, a Byzantine Ballad', Keith Sinclair, *William Pember Reeves: New Zealand Fabian* (Oxford, 1965), pp. 328, 331, 321. Pember Reeves was the author of an Anglo-Hellenic League pamphlet, *An Appeal for the Liberation and Union of the Hellenic Race* (London, 1918).
5. These, some 50 in number, are conveniently listed in Glasgow, op.cit., pp. 284–6.
6. The *Unity of the Greece Race* (London, 1919), pp. 11–12, reprinted from the *Contemporary Review*, February 1919.
7. *Hellas and the Balkan Wars* (London, 1914), p. 308. In the last decade of the nineteenth century, two teachers of Modern Greek had been appointed at King's College: Michael Constantinides and Anastasius Nicholas Dendrino.
8. Andreades to Burrows, 20 Feb. 1915 (K). The following abbreviations are used to denote the whereabouts of particular documents: (G) Gennadius Papers, Gennadius Library, American School of Classical Studies, Athens; (K) King's College London Archives; (S) Subscribers' Committee Papers (Department of Byzantine and Modern Greek Studies, King's College London); (S-W) Seton-Watson Papers; (T) Toynbee Papers, Bodleian Library, Oxford; (U) University of London Archives. Particular documents are to be found in more than one of the above collections. In such cases only one location is given.
9. Miller's *Greek Life in Town and Country* (London, 1905) is one of the most perceptive books ever written about Modern Greece. He was also an authority on the Frankish period, his *The Latins in the Levant: a history of Frankish Greece 1204–1566* (London, 1908) being followed by *Essays on the Latin Orient* (Cambridge, 1921).
10. Andreades to Burrows, 22 May 1915 (K).
11. Burrows to Andreades, 16 Sept. 1915; Andreades to Burrows, 30 Sept. 1915 (K).
12. Gennadius, a leading protagonist in the foundation and early history of the Koraes Chair, passed virtually the whole of his lengthy diplomatic career in England and had been successively and intermittently *chargé d'affaires* and minister in London since 1875. He was last appointed minister in 1910. See Francis R. Walton, 'Portrait of a bibliophile xii: Joannes Gennadius, 1844–1932', *The Book Collector*, xiii (1964), pp. 305–26.
13. Gennadius to Burrows, 2 Oct. 1915; Burrows to Gennadius, 4 Oct. 1915 (S).
14. See C.M. Woodhouse, 'The offer of Cyprus' in the forthcoming proceedings of the First Anglo-Greek Historical Colloquium, Salonica 1983, to be published by the Institute for Balkan Studies.
15. Glasgow, op.cit., p. 251.
16. Ibid., pp. 242ff. Venizelos' letter asking Burrows to represent the Salonica government was dated 30 November 1916. In a postscript, dated 3 December, written immediately after detachments of French and British troops, landed in Athens to enforce Entente demands against King Constantine's government, had been repulsed with serious casualties, Venizelos wrote: 'the bloody events of the last two days ... in Athens ... are enough to

reveal even to the most blind all the frightfulness of King Constantine's true disposition'.
17. *A Short and Easy Modern Greek Grammar ... After the German of C. Wied* (London, 1910).
18. Mary Gardner to Burrows, 11 and 30 Oct. 1915 (K).
19. The history of the Greek community in Britain during the nineteenth and early twentieth centuries is a neglected topic but a brief outline is given in Theodore E. Dowling and Edwin W. Fletcher, *Hellenism in England. A Short History of the Greek People in this country from the Earliest Times to the Present Day ...* (London, 1915).
20. Theophilatus to Burrows, 23 May 1916. On 23 November 1917 G.N. Lykiardopulo wrote to Nicholas Eumorfopoulos that he was very pleased to hear that Venizelos was supporting the chair and was pleased to inform him that he could now definitely promise £1,000 towards the endowment (S).
21. D.J. Cassavetti was an enthusiastic advocate of the adoption of the ethos of the British public school system in Greece: 'it is the physical and moral education of the Public School that the Greek needs'. He believed it unfortunate that it was 'the excitable coffee-house politician' who had come to be looked upon as the representative Hellene, whereas temperamentally it was the *evzone*, the kilted Greek soldier, 'with his manliness and his jolly but courteous ways', who was the counterpart of the English public schoolboy: *Hellas and the Balkan Wars*, pp. 263, 305–6.
22. Presumably Euphrosyne Kephala, the author of *The Church of the Greek People, Past and Present* (London, 1930).
23. As a copy of this letter is to be found in the King's College archives it was presumably sent by Cassavetti to Burrows.
24. Burrows to Helena Schilizzi, 13 July 1916; Cassavetti to Schilizzi, 14 July 1916; Cassavetti to Burrows, 14 July 1916 (K).
25. Burrows to Hartog, 17 July 1916; Hartog to Burrows, 18 July 1916 (K).
26. It was in the Great Hall at King's College that Professor T.G. Masaryk, subsequently President of the newly established Czechoslovak republic, had on 19 October 1915 delivered his influential lecture on 'The Problem of the Small Nations in the European Crisis', inaugurating the newly founded School of Slavonic Studies at the college.
27. Miller to Burrows, 19 Sept. 1916; Burrows to Miller, 25 Sept. 1916; Miller to Burrows, 5 Oct. 1916 (K).
28. Eumorfopoulos to Mitaranga, 1 March 1917 (K).
29. Burrows presumably had in mind people such as Christos Kessary, a young journalist in London. In the summer of 1917 he had asked him to teach Modern Greek on behalf of the War Office during the 1917–18 session in succession to Mary Gardner. Though Kessary had no degree, he did have the certificate of the Corfu gymnasium, 'equivalent I think to Eton or Harrow Colleges': letter from Kessary to Burrows, 26 July 1917 (K). In 1917 it appears that some teaching in Modern Greek was carried out at the college by Dr J.P. Chrysanthopoulos, who presumably did not fall into this category.
30. Although this is precisely what did happen when the conditions attaching to the endowment were revised after Toynbee's resignation.
31. Burrows to Mitaranga, 7 March 1917 (S).
32. He also endowed similar chairs at the Universities of Paris and Petrograd, together with chairs in English Literature at the Sorbonne in honour of Field Marshal Earl Haig and in French Literature at the University of Oxford in honour of Marshal Foch. Oxford duly rewarded Zaharoff with an honorary degree: Donald McCormick, *Pedlar of Death. The Life of Sir Basil Zaharoff* (London, 1965), p. 165.
33. In the preface to Polybius, *Greece Before the Conference* (London, ?1919), p. vii.
34. This meeting, held on 16 November 1917, had been organized on behalf of the Anglo-Hellenic League by Burrows, who had mobilized King's College students to act as stewards. The meeting attracted a huge crowd with thousands being turned away but fell short of the 'monster meeting' which Nicholas Eumorfopoulos had envisaged, Eumorfopoulos to Burrows, 27 Nov. 1917 (K). The Lord Mayor took the chair and the speakers were A.J. Balfour, the Foreign Secretary, Lord Curzon, Winston Churchill, Minister of Munitions, Venizelos, Gennadius and Burrows (Glasgow, op.cit., p. 262).
35. Burrows to Zaharoff, 19 June 1917; Mitaranga to Burrows, 3 Oct. 1917; Burrows to Zaharoff, 29 Dec. 1917 (K).

36. Burrows to Eumorfopoulos, 28 Nov. 1917; Burrows to Mitaranga, 28 Jan. 1918 (K).
37. Interestingly, the first incumbent of the Camoens Chair of Portuguese, which was established at King's College in the same year as the Koraes Chair (1919), was Sir George Young, who is better known for his monumental codification of Ottoman Law published as the *Corps de Droit Ottoman* (Oxford 1905–6, seven volumes) than for his work in Portuguese studies. He was also the author of *Constantinople* (London 1926). His views on the Toynbee controversy do not appear to be on record.
38. Eumorfopoulos to potential subscribers, 22 Dec. 1917 (S).
39. *Ephimeris ton Syzitiseon tis Voulis*. 7, 9 October (OS); *Ephimeris tis Kyverniseos*, 21 November 1917 (OS). I am grateful to Susannah Verney for verifying this information for me.
40. Burrows' circular letter, 3 Jan. 1918 (K).
41. Burrows to Cooper Perry, 7 Jan 1924 (U).
42. In fact the Greek government subsidy was not continued after the controversy had broken out over the chair.
43. Burrows to Hambledon 28 Feb. 1918 (K). This letter appears to have been copied to all members of the college sub-committee appointed to discuss the conditions governing the chair. See Burrows to R.W. Seton-Watson of the same date (S-W).
44. Hambledon to Burrows, 2 March 1918; Edgar to Burrows, 2 March 1918; Busk to Cooper Perry, 3 March 1918 (K).
45. (S).
46. Cooper Perry to Burrows, 25 Feb. 1918 (K).
47. Burrows to Ionides, 11 March 1918 (K).
48. Burrows to Ionides, 13 March 1918 (K).
49. Eumorfopoulos to the Delegacy of King's College, 24 April 1918 (K). The key stipulation was finally formulated thus: if 'a holder of the said Professorship vacates his office for any reason' the Committee shall within two months from the date of receiving notice from the university duly consider 'whether it wishes any changes in the administration of the income of the said fund or the conditions of the next professorship, or whether it wishes to withdraw the fund from the control of the university'. Agenda of Subscribers' Committee meeting 31 July 1918 (S).
50. Eumorfopoulos to Burrows, 24 April 1918 (K).
51. Eumorfopoulos to Burrows, 22 April 1918; Eumorfopoulos to John Mavrogordato, 10 March 1918 (K).
52. Undated (1918) draft indenture between Burrows, A.C. Ionides, N. Eumorfopoulos and the London, County and Westminster Bank (K).
53. A.C. Ionides, in particular, had been unhappy about tying up the trust funds in the way that the university had wished. He disapproved of funding 'a perpetual Chair of Modern Greek which may be quite unsuitable 200 years hence', Eumorfopoulos to Burrows, 14 March 1918 (K).
54. Burrows to Perry and Busk, 26 April 1918; Busk to Burrows, 28 April 1918; Eumorfopoulos was not happy with Busk's objections, supposing that 'Busk considers himself a kind of tin god', Eumorfopoulos to Burrows, 7 May 1918 (K).
55. Burrows to Eumorfopoulos, 19 Feb. 1918; Eumorfopoulos to Burrows, 14, 17 Feb. 1917 (K).
56. University of London Senate Minutes, 15 May 1918.
57. Burrows to Hartog, 17 July 1916 (K).
58. Burrows to Platt, 30 Jan. 1918 (K).
59. Hill to Eumorfopoulos, 22 May 1918 (K); Perry to Gennadius, 17 May 1918 (U).
60. (K).
61. The principal subscribers were Sir Lucas Ralli (through Venizelos) £2,000; M. Embiricos £1,500; L.M. Messinesi £1,000; Helena Schilizzi £500; P. Zarifi, T.P. Zarifi and M.A. Mitaranga £500; C. Coupa £500; G.B. Zochonis £500 and G. Eumorfopoulos £500. The total raised by May 1918 amounted to £11,000.
62. Burrows to Wickham-Steed, 17 May 1918; J. Webb to Burrows, 20 May 1918. Eumorfopoulos was also disappointed by the attitude of *The Times*: 'it is very unfortunate that the Times is now such a rotten paper, while still regarded as the chief English newspaper': Eumorfopoulos to Burrows, 20 May 1918 (K).

2. The Election

Now that the question of the endowment had been settled, Burrows was free to concentrate on the search for suitable candidates for the chair and for the lectureship. He seems to have taken the view that the purposes of the chair would be best filled by an historian, preferably a modern historian,[1] and he still entertained hopes of persuading William Miller to accept the chair. Accordingly, on 9 May 1918 he wrote once again to Miller in Rome to inform him that the chair would now definitely be established. He had, he said, no right to anticipate the choice of the Board of Advisors but he had little doubt that if Miller were willing to stand then he would be elected. From their earlier correspondence, and from Seton-Watson's recent meeting with Miller in Rome, he gathered that it was still uncertain whether he would agree to stand. For this reason he wished to assure him that the chair was not subject to Greek government control. The routine work would not be excessive as a lecturer was soon to be appointed and he hoped to be able to retain Mrs Ernest Gardner as Honorary Lecturer.[2] Miller would be completely free 'to continue and indeed enlarge on a still higher plane the propaganda work on foreign affairs' in which he was now engaged. 'Indeed the authority of this work would be enhanced by a professorship.' Miller, however, was not to be convinced and on 20 May replied that 'after mature consideration' he regretted that he could not stand, as he had informed Venizelos when he was last in Rome. He was now aged 53 and no one, he believed, should begin an entirely new profession at that age. 'No man makes a career after 50; no man who is ambitious becomes a journalist in England'. Moreover, he had been away from England for 15 years and nearly all his very old friends there were either dead or had disappeared. What was more, he and his wife disliked the London climate and were never well there.[3]

Even after this fairly categorical refusal, Burrows did not finally abandon hope of securing Miller. On 5 June he wrote to him that at its recent meeting the Board of Advisors had 'unanimously and strongly' urged him to approach Miller once again 'on the grounds of public policy' for they felt that 'at the present moment there is absolutely no one living who can support the Chair properly except you'. The only other possibility was F.W. Hasluck, a historian with a wide range of interests in ancient and modern Greece,[4] 'and even he is on a considerably lower level than you are'. He asked Miller to consider the position on a three- or even two-year basis and held out the inducement of an arrangement such as had been concluded with Bernard Pares, Professor of Russian at King's College, who had been given special leave to spend two months a year in Russia over and above the usual vacations. Burrows stressed the respect enjoyed by Miller in the Greek colony in London 'whom your prestige alone can interest practically in the work of the Department'. 'Will you be very unselfish,' he concluded, 'and come and help us?' Miller was not to be moved, however, and replied on 11 June that he could not alter his decision: 'I have always been a solitary *Privatgelehrter* – so far as my modest historical studies are concerned – and know nothing of colleges and the like, except the dim reminiscences of my undergraduate days'.[5]

Burrows, clearly disappointed not to have been able to attract Miller to the chair, now began to take wide soundings among British, Greek and French colleagues and acquaintances about suitable candidates for both the chair and the lectureship. The filling of the latter post, which as Burrows wrote to D.P. Petrocochino was practically in his hands,[6] was to prove relatively straight-forward. The search for a suitable professor, now that Miller had made it quite clear that he was not prepared to stand, was considerably more protracted. Burrows had originally hoped that an appointment to the chair could be made in time for the beginning of the 1918–19 session, that is, to start in October 1918, but the starting date was subsequently set back to January 1919 and finally until October 1919.

On 11 June he wrote to Professors Tsourtis, Khatzidakis, Politis and Andreades in Athens to seek their advice on the two appointments. He made it clear that he would prefer an Englishman as professor, or failing that an eminent Greek 'absolutely in the first rank'. As for the lectureship it was essential that this should be filled by a Greek. He realized that the language question, the interminable and at times violent debate that had exercised the Greek intelligentsia for over a century as to the form of the language appropriate to a regenerated Greece, might cause problems but he did not think that these would be insuperable. Unlike Gennadius, now of course a member of the Board of Advisors, who was a fanatical champion of the *katharevousa*, or 'purified', form of the language, Burrows appears to have been open-minded on the language question. He wrote, for instance, to Yannis Psicharis, as robust a champion of the demotic or popular form of the language as Gennadius was of the artificial *katharevousa*, and who was then teaching at the Ecole des Langues Orientales of the University of Paris, that he could not prophesy what the linguistic tendencies of the newly founded department would be but added that he would not 'feel it incongruous if the holder of the Koraes Chair were to prove an interpreter of Demotic'.[7] Burrows had a great admiration for the Sorbonne school of Byzantine and Modern Greek studies which he considered to be much superior to anything in England[8] and wrote, besides Psicharis, to Professors Charles Diehl, the Byzantinist, and Hubert Pernot, the neo-hellenist.[9]

On 25 June Burrows wrote to Petrocochino that for the post of lecturer it was particularly important that the College should get a 'brilliant young man who would be a good representative of Greek culture and learning'. The only candidates in Britain were either journalists or clerics. The journalists were Christos Kessary and C. Pouptis, the editor of a Greek weekly illustrated journal published in London called *Hesperia*.[10] Gennadius had a low opinion of them. Burrows thought them quite intelligent but not in the least learned or academic and, in any case, they in turn were strongly opposed by Gennadius.

Gennadius's favoured candidate was a young deacon, who had taught at the Rizareion Theological School in Athens. This must have been either the Rev. A. Papakonstantinou, who had studied in the Theological Department at King's while officiating at the Greek Orthodox Cathedral in London, or the

Rev. Hilarion Basdekas, a native of Kastoria, who after studying theology in St Petersburg, had taken a B. Litt. degree at Oxford. Basdekas was also attached to the Greek Cathedral, where, among other activities, he was to found the first Greek boy scout troop in London. His work for a theological degree in St Petersburg had included a 'History and Refutation of the Nonconformists' and his thesis had been on Nikodimos of the Holy Mountain (Nikodimos Agioreitis). Whomever it was, Burrows considered him to be 'quite impossible'.[11]

Among Burrows' Greek contacts, Andreades mentioned, among others, the distinguished Byzantinist Konstantinos Amantos (presumably for the chair), while Professor N.G. Politis put forward (presumably for the lectureship) his son George, who had 'studied in France and Germany and knows English' and was now teaching French in a Greek *gymnasion*.[12] A.J.B. Wace, the archaeologist and ethnographer, suggested Manolis Triandaphyllidis, the very distinguished demoticist, for the professorship, although he believed that his duties in the Ministry of Education would prevent him from applying.[13]

One of the most interesting proposals for the lectureship in Modern Greek to emerge from Burrows' soundings among Greek friends and acquaintances came from Leon Maccas, the Greek diplomat and director of *Les Etudes Franco-Grecques*.[14] In a letter to Burrows of 28 July 1918 Maccas put forward, among other possible candidates, a Greek man of letters '*de l'école d'Alexandrie . . . qui est un esprit remarquable*': a Monsieur Cavafis, about whom further particulars could be sought from M. Synadinos, the president of the Greek community in Alexandria. The long conversations which Maccas had had with this Greek had led him to believe that he would be completely up to the task and what was more, he knew English admirably.[15] Maccas's candidate was the poet Constantine Cavafy. Burrows had clearly never heard of Cavafy, and indeed it would have been extraordinary if he had, for the poet was scarcely known outside the Greek world at this time. Conscientious as ever, Burrows consulted Platon Drakoulis[16] as to who this Cavafy might be. Drakoulis, however, had also clearly never heard of the Alexandrine poet for he replied to Burrows on 19 August 1918 that 'as to Mr Cavafis, I knew Dr Cavafis of St George's Hospital and if the young man is his son he was probably born and brought up in London'.[17] This Dr Cavafis was in fact Constantine Cavafy's cousin. Burrows appears to have taken the matter no further.

Two serious candidates for the lectureship in Greek were to result from Burrows' soundings in France. These were Petro J. Petrides and Lysimachos Oeconomos. Petrides was in his late twenties and had studied at the Zographeion School in Constantinople and subsequently at Robert College in the same city, from which he had taken a BA in 1911. From October 1912 until September 1913 he had served in the ranks of the Greek army and, so he informed Burrows in a letter of 4 September, had 'fought both against the Turk and the Bulgar'. He was highly recommended by H.A. Gibbons, the historian of the early Ottoman Empire and the author of a life of Venizelos, who had been one of Petrides' teachers at Robert College, and also by Hubert Pernot who told Burrows in a letter of 13 September that he would have liked to have found him a position at the Sorbonne.[18] Oeconomos, now aged 23, had left Athens for Paris in 1906 at the age of eleven. In 1912 he had gained the French *baccalauréat* and, in 1913, on returning to Greece he had gained the Greek *baccalauréat* as well. After attending courses at the University of Athens for a few months he had returned to France in October 1913 when he had registered at the Sorbonne. He had acquired the *licence ès lettres* (in classical languages and literatures) in July 1915, followed by the *diplôme d'études supérieures* in 1916.[19] Since then, under the supervision of Charles Diehl, he had been working for a *doctorat de l'université* on 'La vie religieuse dans l'Empire Byzantin au temps des Comnènes et des Anges'.[20] This had achieved a '*mention très honorable*'. Oeconomos was strongly recommended not only by Diehl but also, among others, Psicharis and Platon Drakoulis.[21] In addition, Burrows asked D.J. Cassavetti to make further enquiries on his behalf. Cassavetti duly reported on 29 August that Oeconomos wanted to see the *katharevousa* disappear as soon as possible but that meanwhile he recognized that it must be learnt by anyone who had to write or speak Greek officially. Moreover, he wishes to see the language develop from the *dimotiki* of Vilaras rather than from the more extreme or 'hairy' (*malliari*) form of the language.[22] His weak point, Burrows subsequently wrote in his report to the Delegacy of King's College recommending Oeconomos' appointment, was his knowledge 'of England and English', which he spoke 'correctly but haltingly'.[23]

The only other candidate to be seriously considered for the lectureship was John Mavrogordato, then aged 36, a former King's Scholar at Eton and a classical scholar at Exeter College, Oxford, who was strongly recommended by R.R. Marett of the Department of Social Anthropology of the University of Oxford. In 1913 he had published a book on the Balkan wars.[24] Burrows considered him to be both 'an extremely nice man' and an example of 'the best type of the Anglo-Greek colony'. Owing to 'the possession of private means and natural indolence, he only got a second class at Oxford and has never yet really found his métier'. Although a first-rate scholar, with literary taste and style, his own knowledge of 'the modern tongue' was not profound.[25] Mavrogordato was subsequently to become Bywater and Sotheby Professor of Byzantine and Modern Greek Language and Literature at the University of Oxford.

Burrows always seems to have had a clear preference for Oeconomos for the lectureship, although he hoped that it might be possible to associate Mavrogordato with the department at a later date in an honorary capacity. As he wrote in his report to the Delegacy: 'Paris has a living school of Byzantine and Modern Greek and Mr Oeconomos has had a thorough four years' training in its method. We are attempting to organize at King's the first school of the kind in the United Kingdom and it will be of great advantage to be able to profit by French experience'. Burrows' assurance to Petrocochino that the appointment was virtually in his hands proved to be correct for by the end of September he was writing to Cassavetti that Oeconomos had been 'elected' [*sic*] and that he was already helping him over his difficulties in getting a work permit.[26] Yet it was not until December that he was to arrange for his fellow members on the Delegacy Committee appointed to fill the lectureship (Viscount Hambledon and Professor Walters) to sign the formal report necessary for Oeconomos' appointment to be made official.[27] It appears that none of the candidates had been summoned to interview.

Throughout the summer of 1918 Burrows was also taking advice about suitable candidates for the chair from those with a knowledge of the field and was corresponding with potential applicants. Those he consulted included C.A. Hutton, the acting Secretary, and A.J.B. Wace, the Director, of the British School at Athens; Professor Gilbert Murray, the hellenist, at this time attached to the Board of Education, who, when Professor of Greek, had given Burrows his first academic appointment at the University of Glasgow; Professor Sir J.L. Myres; George Macmillan of the publishing firm; and Herbert Warren, President of Magdalen College, Oxford. Hutton mentioned the names of R.M. Dawkins, C.A. Scutt, H.J.W. Tillyard, A.W. Gomme and W.R. Halliday but considered Halliday, who in fact was to become Principal of King's College in 1928, to be the only possible candidate. According to Hutton, Halliday was a gentleman by birth and education. From an old Devonshire family, he acted 'the young squire' during the vacations. Only his eyesight had prevented him from being a fighting man.[28]

Gilbert Murray passed the news of the establishment of the chair to his son-in-law, Arnold Toynbee. Toynbee in consequence wrote to Burrows, enclosing a summary *curriculum vitae*, on 26 July to ask informally whether it would be of any use for him to stand. In his *curriculum vitae* he laid claim to a fairly thorough knowledge of ancient Greek history; a knowledge of Greece itself and of the colloquial language, although not of contemporary literature; three years' experience of teaching as a fellow and tutor in Ancient History at Balliol College, Oxford; and a general acquaintance with Near Eastern history. If the new post were to be primarily a chair of Modern Greek language then he would not consider himself qualified, but if the professor were to be concerned 'with the common culture from which the various national civilizations of Eastern Europe (and specially of course the Greek) have sprung', then it was possible that he might be qualified to stand, although in any case he would have to wait until the end of the war. In his reply of 30 July Burrows strongly urged Toynbee to put in an application, for it was clear to him that he would be a serious candidate. Moreover, the professor would not be expected to concentrate on the linguistic side which would be left to the lecturer. Toynbee did not reply to this letter until 22 September, explaining that it had taken him some time to make up his mind whether or not to stand. He had been much tempted to do so but on thinking the matter over he felt that he would not be master enough of the subject and, in an interesting prefiguration of his later interests, that he would be drawn 'too much towards the history of the Near East and too little towards modern Greek literature'. Moreover, the holder of the chair should be 'more of an active Philhellene than I feel myself to be'. In any case there were bound to be candidates with much more solid qualifications.

Burrows replied on 24 September that he hoped that Toynbee had not finally made up his mind not to stand. He agreed that the title of the chair was 'enough to frighten anybody, but we are not so foolish as to think that anybody can possibly cover the field'. The net had been spread deliberately wide so that the electors would be able to appoint either an historian or a philologist 'in whichever branch we could find the best man'. The chair had actually been offered to William Miller whom Burrows believed to know nothing about philology or Modern Greek literature.

> It is true that he is a Philhellene, but I see nothing in your writing to cause me any qualms on that score. Indeed I have such confidence in Greece that I have not the least doubt that anyone who seriously studies her history and people will strengthen his sympathetic interest in it.

He could not prophesy the electors' choice but as Hasluck was ruled out on health grounds he considered Toynbee to be a very strong candidate. He very much doubted whether he would again find so good an opportunity for specializing in Near Eastern history. He ended his letter: 'Please change your mind'. Toynbee replied the following day that, without wishing to appear ungracious, he could not do so. 'I still feel that I should not fully fit the chair and might find myself not really fulfilling the intentions of the founders. (And though, as you say, that is the elector's business, it is the candidate's too).'[29]

A dark horse in the race was John Jackson, a one-time fellow of Magdalen College, Oxford who, it seems, had first been brought to Burrows' notice when C. Pouptis, the editor of *Hesperia*, sent some articles published by Jackson to Burrows. Replying on 8 August to Burrows' inquiry about Jackson, Herbert Warren, the President of Magdalen College, wrote of him that he was 'a genius, a sort of second Porson in his gift for Greek of all sorts, and indeed for language and literature generally'. But, he enigmatically added, the reasons for his retirement were peculiar, 'partly health and partly other'. Since then he had lived 'a very retired or recluse life' and, although Warren had of late wished to see him brought back to Oxford and the world, he was doubtful 'whether it would be well to bring him suddenly and straight to London and to so big a post'. On the previous day, 7 August, Warren, then in San Remo, had drafted a letter to Burrows about Jackson which he did not, however, send. Burrows' curiosity had, not unnaturally, been aroused by the letter which he did send, that of 8 August, and he pressed Warren for more information. On 19 October Warren wrote to Burrows enclosing the letter of 7 August, marked 'strictly confidential'. This, Warren added, he had not sent earlier because, on second thoughts, he believed 'it hardly fair to him for me to send it unless he were really to be carefully considered'.

> He is, I think, a very good fellow, and more like a genius among scholars than anyone I have come across, and my impression is now that if he wished to come to London himself he might be trusted, for I have great confidence in his right and generous feeling.

In his strictly confidential letter of 7 August, which he requested Burrows to destroy when he had done with it, Warren repeated that Jackson was 'a modern Porson with Porson's genius for Greek of every sort'. 'In some ways he seemed to me to have a finer edged genius than almost any young man I have come across.' A very poor boy, the son of a small farmer, he had been brought to Queen's College, Oxford, through a north country Exhibition. Under the tutelage of A.C. Clark[30] and others he had come on like a house on fire and had won the Ireland scholarship in 1901[31] and an Open Fellowship at Magdalen College in 1903.

> But he was dazzled by success and lost his head, first as an undergraduate and then when we elected him, and to use the old phrase 'went on the bust'. Fortunately we found it out and stopped him. He took it exceedingly well.

Since then he had lived very quietly and had done 'capital work' for the Oxford University Press. Warren believed that he would do well, 'perhaps brilliantly', but felt that he could not recommend him without telling Burrows of this past.[32] Burrows was clearly impressed by Jackson's credentials and Jackson, although never formally a candidate for the chair, was to remain a possibility throughout the selection process.

In a letter of 9 August 1918 A.J.B. Wace, the Director of the British School at Athens and the author, *inter alia*, of *Nomads of the Balkans: an account of life and customs among the Vlachs of northern Pindus*,[33] wrote in response to Burrows' request for the names of potential candidates. He mentioned as possibilities W.H.D. Rouse, J.S. Lawson, C.A. Scutt, Toynbee, and A.W. Gomme, all of whom had been closely associated with the British School. Among possible British candidates only Dawkins, a former Director of the School, in his opinion really knew Modern Greek well 'from the scientific point of view'.[34] But his interest was 'almost entirely purely philological' and he did not have what he would call 'a historical mind'. Nor, indeed, was he a first-class lecturer. On 20 September Burrows wrote to ask Wace himself to consider applying for the chair. Miller would not come, while F.W. Hasluck, the librarian of the British School and a very considerable authority on post-classical Greece, was ruled out by poor health,[35] while Dawkins, although an admirable philologist, had not offered himself as a candidate. Burrows' personal feeling was that if Wace were to abjure prehistory he would now be 'our best man'. Wace, however, replied that he was much too interested in archaeology to abandon it besides the fact that he was too old to do so. 'The only thing that would attract me is modern Greek history ... but that I can study just as well here and besides I know nothing of it'. Not only did he feel that it would be a gross presumption on his part to stand but, more than this, his duty to the British School tied him to Athens.[36] Shortly afterwards Dawkins, who had already suggested Wace among others as a possible candidate, wrote to Burrows formally to rule out his own candidature.[37]

Burrows also invited Alan Leeper, an Australian diplomat, to stand, but on 24 October Leeper regretfully declined, although Byzantine history had been the subject which from the age of 14 he had always planned to study and explore.[38] Burrows also had some correspondence with C.A. Scutt, a wartime lieutenant, who had been among those associated with the British School at Athens who had been recommended by Wace. On 8 October he wrote to Scutt to ask whether he had a general interest in Modern Greek history and whether 'in the broad sense of the word' he considered himself a philhellene.

> By this, of course, I do not mean praise without criticism, for nothing is more important than criticism, but have you a general sympathy for Greeks as Greeks?

Scutt replied on 10 October that he had a great affection for the peasant Greek, 'who has always shown me great kindness and hospitality'. His spoken Greek was largely demotic and he followed events in Greece 'with strong interest'. Presumably he had some sympathy with the Constantinist viewpoint for he wrote that his defence of Greece's attitude during the war had made him extremely unpopular in the Salonica army. Burrows also wrote to the Rev. G.F. Fisher, the future Archbishop of Canterbury, and at this time headmaster of Repton School, to ask him about Scutt, who had spent some time as a schoolmaster at the school. Fisher had no doubt about his great ability and that beneath a 'somewhat insignificant presence' and 'a vein of buffoonery' there was a 'very good brain'. But as a teacher he did not think him to have been more than a fair success and would not have kept him permanently at the school: 'older staff thought (I think rightly) that he was too much of a "cheap wit". Possibly if he had a set of good false teeth, he might have impressed me more favourably. As it was his very ugly mouth of bad teeth gave him a bad start'.[39]

Towards the end of October a meeting of the Board of Advisors was convened to consider the applications of those who had formally applied for the chair, which had been publicly advertised in the wake of Miller's definitive refusal to stand. Those considered at this meeting were M.J. Acatos, H.I. Bell, C.A. Scutt, Dr J.P. Chrysanthopoulos, J.C. Lawson and Dr L. Belleli. Jason Acatos in his application described himself as an 'Englishman of Greek descent'. Aged 47, he had studied ancient and modern Greek at the Greek College of Chalki[40] and subsequently Oriental Languages at the Imperial Ottoman College. Fluent in several languages, he was now senior modern languages master at King Edward's School, Birmingham. H. Idris Bell worked in the British Museum library and was an expert in the papyrology of Byzantine Egypt. Dr J.P. Chrysanthopoulos had already taught Modern Greek at King's in 1917. J.C. Lawson had been a student of J.S. Blackie, Professor of Greek at the University of Edinburgh during the latter part of the nineteenth century and a keen student of modern Greek matters.[41] During the war, Lawson, a fellow of Pembroke College, Cambridge, had served in the RNVR as a naval intelligence officer.[42] He was the author of *Modern Greek Folklore and Ancient Greek Religion* in which he sought 'to trace the continuity of the life and thought of the Greek people, and to exhibit modern Greek folklore as an essential factor in the interpretation of ancient Greek religion'.[43]

The most eccentric applicant was Dr Lazaros Belleli. He declared that he wished he could have named Gennadius as one of his referees but that when he and M. Stavridi[44] had been appointed as the representatives of the Greek government to the London Congress of Moral Education, Gennadius had done something which 'was not calculated to facilitate our mission and I had to protest against his attitude'. 'Although wronged,' he wrote, 'I did subsequently what was compatible with a man's dignity to get reconciled with him, but I do not know whether my overtures have succeeded.' Describing himself, somewhat confusingly, as 'being a Greek by birth and Italian by family', Belleli submitted an extraordinary 32-page typewritten letter in support of his own candidature. In this he gave a long and rambling account of his views on a number of scholarly matters. Educated in Corfu, Athens and Florence, he had nearly failed his examinations in Italian literature in Florence because he had dared to disagree with the professor's views on Dante. On receipt of his doctorate in philology he had for 28 months been headmaster of the Public Jewish Schools of Leghorn. He had worked extensively on the version of the Pentateuch in colloquial Greek printed with Hebrew characters contained in the Soncino polyglot printed in Constantinople in 1547. He was critical of the transcription of the Dutch scholar D.C. Hesseling[45] and prided himself on having been able through a review to prevent Hesseling from receiving the Zographos prize. He had been considered for the Chair of Hebrew at the University of Athens. He had not been elected but 'a little pamphlet of mine had shown the inadequacy of the other applicants'.[46] Extremely sorry once again to have to play the part of 'the merciless iconoclast', he had exposed the Aramaic papyri of Elephantine as forgeries. He took the view that 'the Greek of Byzantine was infinitely more correct and elegant than the Latin of Rome', a view that should have endeared itself to that fierce *katharevousianos* Gennadius whatever the earlier friction between the two.

It would seem that only Bell and Scutt were summoned for interview at the meeting of the Board of Advisors on 24 October. Burrows knew all the Greek candidates, whom he considered to be hopeless.[47] Scutt, on sick leave from the Salonica front, suffering from a malarial attack 'and quite incapable of any mental effort', appears to have been given a grilling by Gennadius as to his views on the language question. For on being informed by Professor M.C.M. Hill, the Chairman of the Academic Council, of the decision of the Board of Advisors to postpone the election, Scutt wrote on 26 November to Burrows to ascertain whether he should now consider himself out of the running, particularly as he was very much aware that he had made a very poor showing at the interview. Burrows replied two days later that, officially, appointment to the chair was still open 'but there is no harm in my giving you my personal impression that it is not probable that you will be elected to the post'. Burrows added that he imagined that Scutt would have found Gennadius' cross-examination 'rather trying'.

> If you will forgive me saying so, the very fact that the questions he asked seemed to be new to you, suggested what I have often thought on other occasions, that it is a pity that some of you who are out in Greece for a long time at the [British] School or on other service, do not mix a little with educated Greeks as well as with the peasants. If you come to think of it, a foreigner who had no knowledge of England except from the conversation of farm labourers or navvies would get a rather one-sided view of things.

To this Scutt replied on 3 December that Gennadius' cross-examination on the language 'could hardly be new to anyone who has given any time at all to the study of modern Greek'. His own views on the subject were those of the average educated Greek with whom he had come into contact at the University of Athens and elsewhere.

> I have no sympathy with the rabid Malliarists or the extreme Purifiers ... I have never heard university teachers like Hatzidakis and Trianta-phyllides speak in extreme *katharevousa*, but I have often heard the village schoolmaster do so.[48]

Belleli, as might be expected, continued to try to lobby Burrows. On 26 November Burrows wrote to him that he had been sorry to have missed him on the several occasions when Belleli had sought to call on him. But, he added, he would be lacking frankness if he held out any hope of election: 'I think it is practically certain that the Professor elected will be an English-man, if we can find the right man'.[49]

The meeting of the Board of Advisors on 24 October decided not to recommend an appointment and urged that further enquiries be made, with a view to filling the chair from the beginning of the 1919–1920 session. Pending such an appointment, however, according to a printed brochure prepared by the college, Oeconomos, assisted by Mary Gardner and Burrows, was to organize classes on language and literature 'some of them adapted for members of the Greek community, others for English students'. In addition ten lectures were to be given by Professor Simos Menardos of the University of Athens on Modern Greek poetry (for which he was paid £200), six by Professor Charles Diehl, Professor of Byzantine History at the University of Paris, on 'Les causes de la grandeur de Byzance', six by John Mavrogordato on Modern Greek history since the foundation of the King-dom[50] and six by Oeconomos on 'Religious Life in the Byzantine Empire of the twelfth century'.[51] The Greek Minister of Foreign Affairs, Nikolaos Politis, directly interested himself in these interim arrangements. On 5 October he telegraphed Caclamanos, who had replaced Gennadius as Greek minister in November 1918, to say that in an earlier letter he had informed the London Legation that after the definitive refusal of the chair by Miller (who clearly always remained the favoured candidate of the Greek government), the chair *ad interim* had been provisionally assigned to Andreades and Menardos for the current year and asked Caclamanos to ensure that these nominations were accepted by the university. The im-plication of this odd communication is that the Greek government believed itself competent to make such dispositions. On 8 October Caclamanos replied that Gennadius had told him that he had already communicated Burrows' reply to the effect that Politis' proposal would be submitted to the Senate. On the other hand Burrows had categorically told Caclamanos that the presence of Andreades (who was not a Venizelist) was undesirable at this time, for his passive attitude to events in Greece had made him unpopular in Entente circles. Politis replied on 16 October asking Cac-lamanos to get Venizelos to intervene in the matter of Andreades, whose services could be useful in British university circles. 'Our English friends should not be more difficult in this respect than we are,' he pointedly concluded.[52]

It is clear that Gennadius had been particularly impressed by the articles on Modern Greek which Jackson had written for *Hesperia*. These in the view of two Greeks of Burrows' acquaintance appeared to be 'quite the best thing that has been written by an Englishman on the subject'. Moreover, in Burrows' view Jackson treated Modern Greek literature 'from exactly the point of view that would insure the success of our Chair'. Burrows was therefore authorized by the Board of Advisors to make further enquiries about Jackson and wrote once again, on 25 October, to Sir Herbert Warren to ask whether any of his old Oxford friends had been in personal touch with Jackson during the last 10 or 15 years or since he went into retirement and, if so, could they give an assurance 'that Mr Jackson has lived a fairly regular life since that time'. He also wished to know whether 'the irregularities to which he yielded' were of such a character as to provoke 'any serious public scandal which is likely to be revived when he emerges from retirement': 'Did his case, for instance, get into the public press, or has anyone a right to feel personally aggrieved at his conduct?'

Warren replied that he was inclined to think that the reply to Burrows' queries would be favourable but that he would move in the matter with great caution.[53] On 11 November an unidentified correspondent wrote to Burrows that he had had the opportunity to talk about Jackson with Professor Clark, the Corpus Christi Professor of Latin at Oxford, who was of the opinion that 'without exception he is the most brilliant linguist that he has known. He was also a modest retiring and attractive fellow'. Although he did drink as a young fellow, since moving to the country he had been a total abstainer.[54]

Burrows now tried to make direct contact with Jackson, which he was able to do with some difficulty. Jackson, writing from Bridge End House, Caldbeck, Wigton, Cumberland, eventually replied to Burrows on 30 January 1919 that 'after almost striving to delude myself into the belief that I am a fit candidate for the Koraes Chair, I have definitely failed to do so'. He had no first-hand knowledge of Byzantine literature or history, nor was he well qualified in Modern Greek. Given two or three years' notice he might be 'a just possible candidate'. 'At the very utmost' he had 'a fair facility' in reading and writing. In speaking he had had extremely little practice. His reading had been deplorably limited for he could find next to nothing to read in that part of the world. 'On the whole, then, though I shall always be proud that you thought of me in such a connection, I feel it is a matter of conscience not to allow you for once to do a disservice to Greece by securing the wrong man for a Chair whose eponym is Koraes'.[55]

Early in the new year of 1919 Burrows was troubled both by the prospect that Joannes Gennadius, who had recently retired as Greek minister in London, might put himself forward formally as a candidate, and by a forged application purportedly in the name of another septuagenarian Greek, Professor G.N. Khatzidakis. On 29 January he wrote to Pember Reeves, on Anglo-Hellenic League business, adding that 'quite between ourselves, G[ennadius] has been hinting that he would like to be our professor'. A few days later in writing to the publisher George Macmillan he again mentioned

Gennadius' possible candidature: 'Gennadius is a wonderful man but he has been getting very difficult to work with lately and has quarrelled with quite a large number of his colleagues'.[56] Moreover, he was 'a purist of the Purists on the language question'.[57] Fortunately for Burrows the university's retiring age was 65, with the possibility of an extension until the age of 70. At about the same time he received what purported to be an application from Professor G.N. Khatzidakis. Burrows' suspicions were aroused, however, and he showed the letter to Professor Simos Menardos, who at this time was giving a course of lectures at King's. Menardos told Burrows that he thought that the letter was not from Khatzidakis but from an individual who was not right in the head. Khatzidakis, on being approached, directly confirmed to Burrows that this surmise was correct. The letter was not from him but from some lunatic. At the age of 70 he had no intention of applying for the chair.[58]

Early in January 1919 Toynbee wrote to Burrows to ask if the chair were still vacant. Burrows replied on 15 January that he was not too late, for the appointment had been postponed so that suitable candidates might know their minds better. There were two or three candidates being seriously considered and he thought it would be useful if Toynbee were to send three testimonials and supply the names of three other referees. He added that Venizelos had sent him a copy of his memorandum, a good deal of which had appeared in *The Times* of the same morning. This set out the various territorial claims which Venizelos was shortly to put before the Council of Ten at the Paris Peace Conference. Burrows felt that Thrace might prove a snare compared with Asia Minor. He asked Toynbee whether anything was known about the future of Aghia Sophia: 'the High Church over here are very keen on the subject'.[59] Toynbee replied on 21 January that he was glad to know that the chair was still open and that he would be writing to his father-in-law, Gilbert Murray, to the Master of Balliol, A.L. Smith, and to J.W. Headlam-Morley, his immediate chief at the Foreign Office, for testimonials, while his referees were Sir William Tyrrell of the Foreign Office, A.J.B. Wace, the Director of the British School at Athens and M.J. Rendall, headmaster of Winchester College, his old school. The Foreign Office were hoping to keep some kind of lien over him, were he to be elected. But he had made it clear that if he were successful he would be at the disposal of the university and could only do other work in so far as this did not interfere with the work of the chair. But the experiment, he thought, might be worth trying.

As to the Venizelos memorandum Toynbee took it to be a maximum programme as it went a good way beyond what he understood he had proposed in conversation. 'Personally,' he added, 'I am pro-Smyrna, and think it will be a great mistake if the Greeks go for Thrace. Thrace is geographically unsatisfactory, and makes good relations with Bulgaria almost hopeless.' He had not been bothering much about St Sophia, which he felt was not really a big question, but it may stand in the way of more important things. 'Couldn't it be securalised, like the Sainte Chapelle has, and become a sort of international monument, under the care of the League?' A week later Toynbee wrote to Burrows that he had spent an hour that afternoon discussing various Greek questions 'with maps and figures' with Venizelos.[60] The main purpose of his letter, however, was to say that he had been thinking about the chair along the lines he had discussed with Burrows the previous summer. If elected he would inevitably develop the historical side: '. . . I should never, I am pretty sure, become a Byzantinist of the detailed wissenschaftlich type, and should always tend to treat the subject broadly – I should be more likely to write a history of East European civilisation than to edit texts or discover new facts'. He believed that it would be important, besides keeping in touch with the Greek colony in England, to travel regularly for at least two months a year to Constantinople (where he hoped some kind of British equivalent to the Russian Archaeological Institute might be founded), Athens and Anatolia. The Foreign Office wanted him to go on working for them 'and though routine work wouldn't be compatible with a professorship, I could probably keep *au courant* with the political intelligence side and might possibly do my travelling on their behalf. I think the travelling is important – it is a pity the long vacation is in the summer, for travelling in the cool weather might be hard to fit in with keeping terms'.[61]

On 3 February Gilbert Murray wrote to Burrows to enclose a testimonial for Toynbee which was 'nothing like so strongly worded as it would have been if he had abstained from entering my family'. At the same time he asked Burrows if he had heard anything of a project for the foundation of a Greek university in Constantinople, which was being advocated by Simos Menardos and C. Pouptis, the editor of *Hesperia*. 'If so, how far do you think they have the right men behind them? The idea in itself seems thoroughly good, and they have been to see [J.B.] Bury and me and, I think, also [Lord] Bryce.' 'The same two people,' he added, 'are proposing to found a society for putting an end to the Turkish Empire, which again is an admirable plan. But do you know anything about it?'

Burrows replied that he had seen Menardos and Pouptis about the proposed University of Constantinople. He believed it to be a promising idea which would, if political events moved the right way, gain the support of rich Constantinopolitan Greeks.[62] But 'from our own point of view it is not so urgent as the scheme, which I daresay you have heard of, of founding schools with some English traditions in them in Greece itself and a kind of Robert College for the Balkans as a whole at Salonika'. As for the proposed society for the destruction of the Turkish Empire he believed this to be a worthy object but thought that there was scarcely time to found such a society before the Peace Conference decided the question. He went on to say that a society, under the presidency of Lord Bryce, had been founded for the return of Aghia Sophia to the Orthodox faith.[63] This movement had weighty support from both the Church (of England) and the Non-Conformists, although the Roman Catholics were violently opposed to the idea. Burrows had very much encouraged the movement as it was 'a sound and useful method of gathering new supporters for the policy of turning the Turkish government out of Constantinople'.[64]

In his testimonial for Toynbee, Murray expressed the hesitation he felt in writing on behalf of someone to whom he was related by marriage. But he still thought that Toynbee possessed some remarkable qualifications as a candidate for the Koraes Chair.

> As a historian he stands in the very front rank of the younger historians produced by Oxford . ... There can be no doubt of his being a man of striking and unusual powers of mind . ... I think his combination of knowledge, linguistic and historical, past and present, with political insight and originality of mind is of a kind very rarely met with.

On 27 January, J.W. Headlam-Morley, the assistant director of the Political Intelligence Department of the Foreign Office, had written to Burrows that, like all his other colleagues, he had been greatly impressed by Toynbee's great industry and intellectual power, while on 2 February A.L. Smith, Master of Balliol College, Oxford, of which Toynbee had been a fellow between 1912 and 1915, wrote on his behalf. He had been an exceptionally successful lecturer, attracting one of the largest audiences for his lectures on Greek history. With his 'extremely alive mind' he was 'always intensely interested in anything he is doing and has the power of communicating that interest to others.' '. . . He has an infectious enthusiasm, which is so much in a teacher.' There was '. . . something very fine and something very engaging and attractive about him. In both these respects he always reminded me very much of his uncle[65] and namesake . . .'. On 7 February M.J. Rendall, who had been Toynbee's headmaster at Winchester, wrote to Burrows to say that Toynbee had been '. . . full of learning, but without a trace of priggishness'.

> What strikes one most about him intellectually is, firstly, his broad grasp of any subject which he tackles; and secondly, his untiring love of study. He is, in all senses of the word, a progressive man.

On 15 February, A.J.B. Wace, the Director of the British School at Athens, wrote to Burrows that he had known Toynbee since 1911 when they had been fellow students at the School. He considered Toynbee 'a sound scholar and a historian of considerable promise'. 'A very hard worker' endowed with 'unbounded energy and enthusiasm' his election would 'give him the opportunity of infecting other students with his enthusiasm for Hellenism'. Wace believed that whoever was appointed should be made to spend plenty of time in the Greek lands, for Greece was a country that it was very easy to get out of touch with. He thought that it might be an idea for the Koraes Professor to change places every three or four years with a professor at the University of Athens.[66]

Toynbee also submitted at this time a detailed *curriculum vitae*. Now aged 29, he had been a scholar of Winchester between 1902 and 1907 and a scholar of Balliol between 1907 and 1911. He had been Jenkyns Exhibitioner at Balliol and Craven Scholar in 1910, the year in which he had gained a first in Mods, and in the following year he had gained a first in Literae Humaniores or Greats. From 1912 to 1915 he had been a fellow and tutor in Ancient History at Balliol College. He had been rejected as unfit for military service both before and under the Derby scheme.[67] In 1917 he had been classed CI but had been retained by the Foreign Office. From 1915 to 1917 he had worked at Wellington House and in 1917–18 in the Department of Information. He had joined the Political Intelligence Department of the Foreign Office in 1918 and had been a member of the British Delegation at the Paris Peace Conference. He wrote that his colloquial Modern Greek which had been fluent in 1912 was now rather rusty and that he had been learning Turkish for a year. Among his already formidable catalogue of publications he listed his article on 'The Growth of Sparta';[68] his pamphlet on *Greek policy since 1882*;[69] his section on Greece in the collective volume *The Balkans*;[70] *Nationality and the War*;[71] *The New Europe: some essays in reconstruction*,[72] a series of essays most of which first appeared in the magazine *Nation*; his compilation of evidence for the Blue Book on *The Treatment of Armenians in the Ottoman Empire, 1915–1916*;[73] a half-written volume on the *History of Ancient Greece* for the Home University Library and various articles on Pan-Turanianism, the future of Turkey and Asiatic Russia.[74]

In his reply to Murray's letter of 3 February Burrows had said that the choice of the new professor would really lie between Toynbee and one other man. This was A.W. Gomme, then aged 32 and since 1911 a lecturer in Greek at the University of Glasgow. A major scholar of Trinity College, Cambridge, he had gained first-class honours in both parts of the Classical Tripos. He had spent the academic year 1908–09 as Prendergast Scholar at the British School at Athens. Before going to Glasgow he had been assistant lecturer in classics at the University of Liverpool. He had spent five weeks in Greece in the spring of 1913. In the course of the war he had passed nine months in Macedonia in 1915–16 and a longer period in Athens and Constantinople in 1918 in connection with his military duties. He listed as his principal publications two articles on 'The topography of Ancient Thebes' and 'Ancient Trade Routes in Boeotia' in the *Annual of the British School at Athens*[75] and on 'The Legend of Cadmus, and the Logographi' in the *Journal of Hellenic Studies*.[76] His referees were G.A. Davies, Professor of Greek at the University of Glasgow, E. Harrison, a fellow of Trinity College, Cambridge and the hellenist Professor Sir J.L. Myres, then serving in the British Legation in Athens. On 11 March Myres sent a reference for both candidates to the Academic Registrar. Of Gomme he wrote that he had

> given much attention to modern Greek Literature, especially to romance, poetry and drama. Greek acquaintances in Athens have expressed to me very favourable opinions of his knowledge and judgement. He has followed carefully the current controversies as to standards of Greek speech and style, in their educational aspects. His natural bent is towards criticism and discussion; he is a good debater, but he does not at present write readily or fully; but he has made positive contributions to the geography and archaeology of the country, and has shown that he knows how to present his materials when required.

In the same letter Myres wrote of Toynbee that his

interests are rather historical and social. He has made a special study of the relations of Balkan peoples to each other and to their geographical and economic surroundings. He reads and speaks modern Greek, but he is more attracted by the people themselves and their doings than by their literature. He has lectured in Oxford on the ancient history and geography of Greece, and also on the social structure of Greece at all periods. He is a good speaker and a most stimulating teacher, full of energy and ideas, and quick to grasp the bearing of new material. He has already published essays on modern history, and questions of European politics.[77]

Burrows was somewhat puzzled by Myres' testimonial for it appeared to him to rank Gomme first, yet when Burrows had last seen Myres, as he wrote to him on 18 March, he had used 'the remarkable phrase "Toynbee begins where Gomme ends"'. He had interpreted this to mean that Toynbee was the candidate of greater ability and promise. The following day Myres replied that he was sorry that his letter had proved such an oracle. What he had meant to convey was that

for this appointment, Gomme has the advantage of a more formal training, more critical temper. He is and will remain a thoroughly good teacher and researcher, but I should not back him for more. Toynbee, with less special knowledge, has already a wider outlook, and would appeal to a wider circle. Though he is a first-class teacher, I doubt whether he will be content to remain a teacher only or always, and I was at first surprised to hear that he was a candidate for a teaching post at all. His interest in Greek things seems to me to be rather a means than an end, and within the subject itself, his interest is rather in the interpretation of movements than in the collection of materials. That is what I wished to express by the phrase which you quote.

As far as intellectual ability went he did not feel that there was very much to choose between the two, the essential contrast lay in their point of view. 'To put it another way, Gomme is a first-rate classical scholar of the Tripos type; Toynbee is an "alpha" Greats-man'.[78]

Toynbee, and presumably also Gomme, attended for interview on 24 March. The Board of Advisors were unanimous in recommending that Toynbee be appointed and that same evening R.W. Seton-Watson un-officially told him that he had been provisionally elected. Whereupon Toynbee immediately wrote to Burrows to say that, while he was very much looking forward to the job, he felt that he must write forthwith to make clear his position on a point that had arisen in the interview, otherwise he would feel that he 'had been elected under false pretences to a certain extent'. He felt unable to undertake to acquire a deep enough knowledge of Greek to enable him to give lectures on language and literature. To do so would take up so much time over so many years that it would almost cripple his work on the historical and political side 'on which my aptitude lies and for which all my previous study and experience have fitted me'. He hoped that this would not lead to the decision of the Board of Advisors being rescinded but he felt very strongly that he ought not to undertake an obligation which might spoil the work he believed himself capable of doing. This letter crossed with one written by Burrows on the same evening, informing him of the decision of the Board and asking Toynbee that, before the next session, he should spend as much time as possible reviving his Modern Greek and reading Modern Greek literature. A large number of his students would be from the Greek colony in London and it was important that he should be able to understand them 'on difficult subjects beyond the range of the vocabulary one uses with a peasant'. He ought to be able, if necessary, to make a speech in Greek. But the Greeks in England were quite reasonable, 'and you need not be alarmed at the standard expected'.

On the following day, 25 March, Burrows, having received Toynbee's letter of the previous evening, hastened to reassure him that he need have no qualms about the linguistic aspects of the job.[79] The first man that had been thought of for the post, William Miller, was quite as much of an historian and publicist as Toynbee but less of a philologist. 'The subject is an immense one, and if you specialise in History and Politics it will be enough. What I have been thinking of is not specialism in Language or Literature, but sufficient familiarity with them to give the Greeks confidence in you'. To this Toynbee replied that he proposed to spend the winter term in Greece improving his Greek.[80] On 25 March Burrows also wrote a sympathetic letter to Gomme, informing him that he had not been successful.[81] Gomme had a distinguished career as a classical scholar and retained his Modern Greek interests, writing a short but informative book on Modern Greece, entitled *Greece* (London, 1945).

Toynbee's tenure of the chair was to begin on 1 October 1919, the income from the endowment during the academic year 1918–19 being used to pay for the lectures by Diehl, Menardos and Mavrogordato and to build up the departmental library, to which Gennadius gave generously. On 17 April, Toynbee asked whether he might be granted permission to miss the first term to act as the secretary to the proposed Inter-Allied Commission on Mandates in Turkey (out of which the King-Crane Commission developed) which it was proposed should visit the territories to be detached from the Ottoman Empire. On 19 April Burrows replied that he was somewhat worried at the prospect of Toynbee not being at the college for the first term, as he had had experience of others being kept on war service. There was, moreover, a further 'more subtle point which may or may not be valid'.

> It is hardly likely that the Commission will entirely satisfy Greece. That is no reason whatever why you should not accompany it and advise it but it might be a useful loophole for you not to be with it to the very end. It will always be possible for them to think what might have been! The only counter-balancing *pro* that I can see is that if you fear that the Commissioners will be pro Turkish and that your presence is really vital for the Greek and Armenian races.

Burrows was anxious for Toynbee to be in residence by the end of October unless there were important political considerations preventing this. He concluded by asking Toynbee whether he could tell him anything about what was being proposed at the Peace Conference for Smyrna.

Toynbee replied on 22 April that, although he had been appointed secretary of the Commission, there was now no need for him to miss the first term. As to Burrows' query about Smyrna he answered:

> Smyrna is a geographical conundrum – and I see no solution for the Greek and Armenian diaspora in Anatolia, which is bound to exist in every Anatolian town so long as the Turk doesn't learn professions or trades. For the sake of the diaspora, I hope the mandatory system will be extended to what is left of Turkey, as well as to the new states.

Toynbee did not tell Burrows of his growing doubts as to the viability of the Greek claim to the Smyrna region. For it was in mid-April that Toynbee and Harold Nicolson plotted together a possible solution to the thorny problem of Constantinople and the Straits.

> As we have demobilized so quickly … we shall be unable to put the Greeks into Smyrna. I mean keep them there. They can't hold it without allied support or unless the whole of Turkey behind them is split up among the Allied Powers. Yet if they do not get Smyrna Venizelos will fall from power. We agree, therefore, to propose to cut the Gordian knot. Let the Turks have Anatolia as their own. Give the Greeks European Turkey only.

'All other solutions,' they argued with considerable prescience, 'would entail trouble in the future.'[82]

In the first prefiguration of his later problems over the chair Toynbee added that he had been shaken to hear that the Greek donors of the Koraes fund had 'turned me down because they wanted a professor who specialised in the Modern Literature'. In a pencilled note on Burrows' reply to this letter, dated 25 April, Toynbee wrote that after the election he had been told casually by the archaeologist D.G. Hogarth in Paris that he had heard that the donors had been dissatisfied with his appointment. Toynbee had therefore written to ask Burrows if this were true and what the position of the donors was. Burrows replied that he did not know what Toynbee's informant could possibly have meant.

> The donors have no say in the matter at all, even if they had wanted to, which I am convinced they do not. The report of the Board of Advisors is coming up in due course [for ratification by the Senate], and I have no doubt about the result.

Toynbee had subsequently noted: 'Would not anybody suppose that this meant that the control had finally passed out of their hands, and not that they would have control at a later stage?'[83] What is somewhat puzzling, however, is that Toynbee appears to have been unperturbed by the presence on the Board of Advisors for the chair of the former Greek minister, Gennadius, a man of strong and forthrightly expressed views who, as we have seen, by no means played a passive role in the selection process and who had such pronounced views on the language question. What Toynbee did not know was that Gennadius, besides his diplomatic connections, enjoyed a preponderant role in the Subscribers' Committee. Nor, at this juncture, was he even aware of the Committee's existence.

On 29 May 1919 the Academic Registrar of the University of London, P.L. Hartog, wrote to Toynbee to inform him that the Senate had confirmed his appointment to the Koraes Chair of Modern Greek and Byzantine History, Language and Literature. He was to have the title of 'Koraes Professor of Modern Greek in the University of London' and was to be appointed a member of the Boards of Studies in Classics, History and Archaeology, in accordance with Senate Minute 2180 of May 1918. This minute contained no mention of the Subscribers' Committee. On Hartog's letter Toynbee subsequently pencilled that 'this letter and enclosures were all that I knew about the conditions of the Chair until February 1923, at which date I learnt for the first time 1) of the existence of a permanent committee of Subscribers 2) of the powers conferred upon this Committee by Senate Minutes 2171–9 and 2181–2, which have never been communicated to me'. A further pencilled note reads: 'On receiving this communication, could anyone dream that there were other and vital conditions attached to the tenure and administration of the Chair, which had not been communicated? AJT'.[84] Minute 2171 contained a copy of Eumorfopoulos' letter of 24 April 1918 to the Delegacy of King's College, which included the Subscribers' 'wish' that the university should provide the Committee with an annual scheme of work, together with a triennial report.

On 27 May, the day before the Senate had formally ratified his appointment, Toynbee had written to Burrows to say that for the moment he was crocked up: 'I suppose one would call it a mild breakdown, overwork being the cause and my typhoid inoculation finishing me off'. He had been forbidden by his doctor to accompany the Inter-Allied Commission and ordered to go off to the country and do nothing for the summer. The next day Burrows wrote to notify Toynbee that his appointment had been duly ratified, and adding that he was very sorry to learn that Toynbee had overdone it but not surprised in view of the strain he had gone through. On 2 June, Toynbee's wife, Rosalind, wrote to Burrows to say that her husband's slight breakdown was showing signs of mending slowly but that he was worried by the thought that he might not be fit enough to take up the professorship by the autumn, although she herself felt that he would be better by then. Burrows on 5 June sympathetically assured Mrs Toynbee that there was no cause for either of them to be anxious and that he was confident that by September he would feel quite a different man.[85] In fact Toynbee appears to have made a quick recovery, for already by the middle of July he was writing to R.W. Seton-Watson to say that he was submitting an article to *The New Europe*.[86] Three weeks later he wrote, from Castle Howard, his mother-in-law's ancestral home, to Seton-Watson to say that he was making good progress 'playing tennis most of the day and not minding much what happens anywhere else ...'[87]

On 16 May Burrows had written to Toynbee to give his blessing to Toynbee's teaching plans and about the building up of a library for the newly established department, adding in conclusion that 'as you can well imagine I am delighted about Smyrna'.[88] The news that so delighted Burrows was obviously that of the landing the previous day, with the encouragement of Britain, France and the United States and under the protection of their fleets, of Greek troops in Smyrna. Smyrna and its hinterland, with its substantial Greek population, had long been one of the most cherished of Greek irredenta. Britain and France broadly supported Greek claims to the Smyrna region, the United States was more doubtful and Italy, which had its own territorial ambitions in Asia Minor, flatly opposed them. Although doubts had begun to emerge as to whether a Greek presence in Western Asia Minor could be sustained the landings had been authorised by the Supreme Council to pre-empt Italian attempts to move northwards from the Antalya region towards Smyrna. The ostensible pretext for the landing was the need to protect the Christian populations of the area, pending the determination of the peace settlement for the Ottoman Empire. The landings on 15 May gave rise to serious incidents involving Greek occupation troops and the local Turkish population. More than 100 Turks were killed, including a number of soldiers shot by their Greek guards after they had been taken prisoner. The Greek authorities acted drastically, if somewhat belatedly, against the perpetrators, and two offenders, including a Greek soldier, were court-martialled and shot as a consequence. None the less, from the outset these incidents were fatally to compromise Greece's 'civilizing mission' in Asia Minor and the landings were to act as a powerful catalyst for the development of the Turkish national movement under the leadership of Mustafa Kemal (Atatürk).[89]

Burrows' own reaction to these events indicates that there were limits even to his philhellenism. On 21 June he wrote to Venizelos to report on an interview he had been given at the Foreign Office in connection with the incidents accompanying the Greek landing. He had written to the Foreign Office to say that he had seen the Greek telegrams on the events but that before taking the matter up he wished to know what information there was from British sources. At the Foreign Office interview extracts had been read out from Admiralty reports and 'the impression they had left on the Foreign Office was deplorable'. They attached no importance to the looting in the night, but laid stress on the *evzonoi* getting out of hand when escorting the prisoners from the barracks to the ships and *'themselves taking part in the killing of men who had surrendered'*. Burrows had said that the Greek account referred to the crowd and had suggested that this might have been the source of the violence. To this the answer had been that it had been the escort itself that had been responsible and that the officers had lost control. 'One sentence read out to me was this. "We were glad to observe *one* Greek officer restraining his men".' His informant at the Foreign Office had said that 'the less said about the matter the better. It was a bad business and has left a bad impression on our men on the spot'. Burrows wanted to know whether English naval officers were themselves in the streets or houses of Smyrna so that their evidence would be first-hand. Or was it possible that they had relied on the word of British residents in the city 'who, as we know, are prejudiced'. Burrows was certain that the last had not been heard of these incidents and all the exact and detailed information that he could secure would be of value. He knew how vexed Venizelos would be. 'Jealous eyes were (and are) watching what occurs in Asia Minor, and it was absolutely criminal of the officers in command if they were as negligent as the Foreign Office believes, even granting Turkish provocation.'

A week later, Burrows again wrote to Venizelos about a further interview he had had with the Foreign Office. On leaving his informant had said, 'This is the end of the Turks being turned out of Europe. There is not a chance of it now'. Burrows had asked whether he had meant only Constantinople or Thrace also, whereupon he had replied 'Oh! Thrace and everything'. Burrows suspected that these remarks represented the views of the Foreign Secretary, Lord Curzon. He feared that these views would be increasingly shared and that they would strengthen the old argument that Greece could not be trusted with the governance of the Muslim minority in Cyprus. He feared, too, that the Greek press had got altogether too rosy a view of the situation and advised that it might be well to prepare it to be disillusioned. 'If, which I still pray to be impossible, Greece is to lose politically because of this monetary loss of control at Smyrna, it will be well that the blame should be put on the right shoulders.' He concluded that he was writing nothing until he had got a lead from Venizelos. Venizelos replied on 9 July that he had heard of the shooting of prisoners by their accompanying guards for the first time from Burrows' letter. He was inclined to attribute the troubles to the worst elements of the population that were not scarce in a large seaport and to the fact that the Turks had thrown open the prisons. But he had asked Colonel Mazarakis, his military adviser 'whom I trust absolutely', to carry out an investigation. He was certain that, even if there had been untoward incidents, the Greek army was conscientiously fulfilling its difficult mission in Asia Minor. He felt confident that, whatever the provocation, the conduct of the Greek soldiers 'has not been more extreme than would have been, under similar circumstances, the conduct of the armies of the majority of the nations foremost in civilisation'. In conclusion Venizelos thanked Burrows for his unceasing concern for the cause of Hellenism which he was sure would not prove unworthy of this interest.[90] It was in the following month, July 1919, that King Alexander, acting on Venizelos' recommendation, made Burrows a Knight Grand Commander of the Order of George I. The Greek minister in London, Dimitrios Caclamanos, wrote to notify Burrows that the decoration had been conferred on him as a token of the government's 'deep gratitude as well as that of the Greek people, for your untiring fervour in defending and promoting the Hellenic cause in your great country'.[91]

As Burrows had predicted, Toynbee was fully recovered by the beginning of the autumn term and duly delivered his inaugural lecture on 'The Place of Mediaeval and Modern Greece in History' in the Great Hall of the College on 7 October 1919, the chair being taken by Joannes Gennadius. Gennadius launched the proceedings with a lengthy introductory peroration. He began by adverting to the presence in the audience of 'the one whose agency has been the most potent in the realization of this foundation', by whom he meant not Burrows but Eleftherios Venizelos, the Greek prime minister, 'our beloved and trusted great Leader, who has transformed our secular dreams into realities, who has raised Greece from ignominy to honour, and who has won for himself and for Greece the appreciation, the respect, and the confidence of the civilized world assembled in Paris'. Gennadius then launched into a lengthy tirade against Gibbon, whom he accused of Mohamedism, Romanism, *suppressio veri* and *suggestio falsi*. He was harshly critical of the depredations of Catholic Christendom at the expense of the Byzantine Empire and argued that the Byzantine Church, 'in saving the world from universal submission to the Papacy', heralded the Reformation, earning on this account 'the remorseless hostility and envenomed calumny of Catholic writers'. More recent scholarship by French and German scholars had abundantly established 'the great superiority of the Byzantines over their western contemporaries'.

It was inevitable that Gennadius would not forgo an opportunity such as this to promote his views on the language question. He argued that it was 'but natural to expect that from a chair dedicated to the memory of Korais, the standard of language to be taught will be that which Korais himself indicated and traced out'. The language of the educated should be taken as the norm, just as the standard of the English language was not to be sought in Petticoat Lane or in the barrack-room. 'It is agreed, if I am not mistaken, that for good and pure English you should listen to Oxford men speaking English.' Gennadius' own command of English, incidentally, was astonishing. Horace Rumbold, a former minister at the British Legation in Athens, declared that Gennadius 'not only spoke, but wrote English more perfectly than almost any other foreigner' he had ever known.[92] Gennadius argued that the Greek language acted as a kind of barometer of the political fortunes of the Greek nation. Whenever Greece was free and prosperous it rose in purity and perfection. 'Barbarism and sordidness were the unmistakeable marks of slavery and abasement.' He continued:

> ... It may be fairly laid down that the standard of the Greek of to-day is the style in which our laws are drawn up, in which our administrative literature is couched, in which the best speakers in the Chamber express themselves, in which the Professors lecture in our gymnasia and in our University, in which the most respectable organs of our Press are written.

He went on to say that he could not conceal the fact that 'some of those who laboured and contributed most to the establishment of this Chair, have given expression to the apprehension lest it should be used as a channel in propagating the queer fancies of Mr Psichari and his concert of sciolist youths'.[93] Such apprehensions, however, appeared to Gennadius to be 'by the very nature of things' unfounded. 'For its realisation would amount to the *reductio ad absurdum* of a chair graced by the name of Korais.' Such a travesty could not be possible when the chair was being inaugurated 'in the presence of him who has been its principal and far-sighted promoter', by whom he again appears to have meant Venizelos rather than Burrows.

Toynbee was somewhat put out by the length of Gennadius' preamble,[94] but went on to give a characteristically wide-ranging and stimulating *tour d'horizon*. He compared the historical experiences of Greece and the West at two critical junctures, the seventh and eighteenth centuries AD, periods in which they were traditionally held most to have diverged from one another. He argued that this traditional view was mistaken and

> that the resemblances between East and West European history are more significant than the differences. We should in fact regard the civilisations of Eastern and Western Europe as organisms which are not merely related to one another by a common parentage, but which have passed, in their growth, through parallel processes of evolution, towards a union as close as that from which they originally sprang.

He concluded the lecture by alluding to the common tasks that lay ahead of Greece and England. The Greek nation state, he argued, was taking the place of the Ottoman Empire as the land-bridge between the Middle East and Europe and, in an interesting prefiguration of one of his major concerns in *The Western Question in Greece and Turkey*, 'Greek statesmen will be exercised by the problem – which Turkey never attempted to solve – of enabling Europeans and Moslems to live together, not only as peaceful neighbours but as members of the same democracy'. England, in turn, if it had no Muslim community to rule over at home, did have the task of ruling huge Muslim populations, separated by thousands of miles of sea. 'We cannot tell,' he concluded, 'which task will prove the more difficult, but one thing is indisputable: we shall have much to learn from one another.'[95]

Burrows appears to have been somewhat concerned that Toynbee's dense argument and his concern with the broad sweep of history might pass over the heads of the students at King's College, for Toynbee wrote to him on 23 October to say that he was grateful for his criticisms of the lecture, which he would pass on to Gilbert Murray for his opinion. He had viewed an inaugural lecture (from hearing them at Oxford) as 'a sort of formal "praelection" – meant to be published and read'. He went on to reassure the Principal that during the course of lectures he was currently giving to undergraduates he was not reading but rather talking from notes, with lantern slides, 'which I think is more on the lines you suggest'. Venizelos, however, had been well enough pleased to tell Gennadius that he thought the lecture should be published.[96] The lecture was duly printed in a run of a thousand copies by S. Vellonis, Ltd., a Greek printer in London, at a cost to the Legation of £1,000.[97]

Burrows must have derived immense satisfaction from the establishment of the chair and from the fact that the first incumbent was so distinguished a scholar as Arnold Toynbee. For among his many innovations at the college without question the establishment of the Koraes Chair lay closest to his heart. In November 1919, however, the month following Toynbee's inaugural, he entered a nursing home where he underwent two operations for cancer. Although he was mortally ill his thoughts during the following months were constantly on Greece. He took particular pleasure in the remarks made by Venizelos to his friend and subsequent biographer, George Glasgow, at the Ritz on 18 February 1920:

> The whole of Greece is watching anxiously for better news of Dr.

Burrows. It is not only that we have in him a devoted friend, but his knowledge of Greece is so great. Quite constantly in reading his articles in the *New Europe* and other papers I learn facts about Greece which I did not know before, and find myself provided with arguments for our cause which I should never have thought of.[98]

One of the last letters that Burrows ever wrote was addressed on his deathbed to Venizelos. Venizelos published this astonishingly moving letter in the foreword which he contributed to Glasgow's memoir of Burrows.[99] So remarkable, however, is this letter, the original of which is to be found among Venizelos' papers in the Benaki Museum in Athens, that it deserves to be reproduced here:

> Principal's House,
> King's College,
> Strand.
> May 5/20

Dear Friend,

So San Remo is over, and all is well! It was like your thoughtfulness to send me that prompt letter in the midst of all your work. Νυν απολυεις τον δουλον σου, Δεσποτα εν ειρηνη οτι ειδον οι οφθαλμοι μου το σωτηριον σου. [Lord, now lettest thou thy servant depart in peace: according to thy word. For mine eyes have seen: thy salvation] Yes, dear friend, I can sing that *nunc dimittis* in all joy and solemnness. This may well be my farewell letter to you. The Doctors tell me that the trouble has broken out again, and that the end may come very soon. I see from a telegram that you are taking back the good news in triumph to Greece.[100] That is your last battle; the recreation of a united Hellas. I have no doubt that you will sweep the polls again at the election,[101] but there is something harder to do, to convert the ignorant, obstinate – often well meaning – folk whose whole outlook was perverted and turned to bitterness by the Royalist struggle. You are still, thank God, young and strong, and you can do such mighty things these next ten years if you have the whole nation behind you. It is not only that I have unbounded faith in you, my Pericles, but I love Hellas as a whole, and I love those dear people, many of them friends of mine in the past, and cannot bear that they should be so blind. Ah well! It may be that your sweet reasonableness will win them in the end. Goodbye, φιλε μου [my friend] and may you and Ελλας [Greece] sometimes think of me

> Ronald Burrows[102]

Burrows' wife, Una, enclosed this letter with a covering note to Venizelos on the next day, 6 May: 'He thinks of Greece all the time. His heart is with you'. Ronald Burrows died on 14 May. The draft of Venizelos' reply to Mrs Burrows, written after he had learnt of Burrows' death, survives among his papers.

No words of mine can adequately express my feelings of sympathy to you, or the deep sorrow I feel at the irreparable loss. He left a vacancy in our hearts which no one else will be able to fill, and his last letter to me is a most eloquent testimony of the great heart and of the noble mind that were his. I wish he could have been spared to visit and see with his own eyes the 'Greater Greece' for which he has worked as few[103] have. He would indeed have experienced the secret satisfaction of knowing that he had not laboured in vain.[104]

Perhaps the best obituary of Burrows was composed by his friend and close collaborator in the foundation of the School of Slavonic Studies, R.W. Seton-Watson. It appeared a few days after his death in *The New Europe*, of which Burrows had been a co-founder with Seton-Watson.

It is difficult to write of so personal a loss as the death of Ronald Burrows: it is still more difficult to believe that so doughty a champion of all the ideals which we exist to promote has passed from us at his very prime. He was one of those who made friends everywhere and who gave them of his best, tireless in well-doing, continually open to new ideas, inspiring others with his own unselfishness and fine enthusiasm. ... No one who had heard it will ever forget his laugh, which seemed the very soul of merriment ...

It was through Greece that he was drawn steadily into the current of Balkan and Central European politics. ... He was eager that the Universities should take the lead in learning and friendly intercourse among the nations. He therefore flung wide the doors of King's College to the exiles of many countries ... The inauguration of the School [of Slavonic Studies] by Professor Masaryk in October 1915 was an event of European significance; the subject of his lecture, 'The Problem of Small Nations', was a challenge to Britain to cast off her insularity, to neglect Europe's race problems at her peril ...

There must always be a certain risk in connecting the academic and political fields; but it is more than ever essential that the task should be undertaken on broad and statesmanlike lines. The work of Burrows at King's College was a first attempt in this direction, and it is to be hoped that others will carry his ideas to fruition.[105]

At Burrows' funeral a magnificent wreath from the Greek government was placed on his grave, inscribed 'To a Great Englishman – a friend who understood, sympathised with, and assisted in the realisation of Greek aspirations – a token of deep and undying gratitude'.[106] A memorial service was held on 6 June at the Greek Cathedral of Saint Sophia in Moscow Road, London, at which the Greek Government, the Greek Legation and the London Greek community paid their respects, while a deputation of Greeks from Constantinople, Pontus and other parts of Asia Minor placed a wreath on the Cenotaph in Whitehall as 'a token of recognition of Dr. Burrows'. In Constantinople, the *Ellinikos Philologikos Syllogos* (Greek Literary Society), the leading Greek cultural body in the Ottoman Empire, which for more than 60 years had been 'the gathering place of all the unredeemed Greeks and the centre of all literary and scientific movement in the East', passed a resolution noting 'the help and inspiration they have gained from the friendship and support of so ardent and sincere a friend and so great a scholar',[107] while in Athens at a meeting of the Greek branch of the Anglo-Hellenic League, D.P. Petrocochino, one of the subscribers to the chair, paid tribute to Burrows. Two years later the Municipal Council of Limassol in Cyprus, in recognition of his efforts on behalf of the *enosis* of Cyprus with Greece, and desirous of expressing 'the gratitude of the citizens of the town', named one of the streets of Limassol after him (Οδος Ροναλδου Μπαρρους).[108] At King's College, the Ronald Burrows Memorial Prize in Greek Studies, to the funding of which an impressively large number of friends and acquaintances of Burrows subscribed, was instituted in his memory. The library of the newly established Department of Byzantine and Modern Greek Studies was named after Burrows and has developed into incomparably the richest library in the field in any British university. It constitutes indeed a fitting memorial to a man of remarkable qualities, both academic and personal.[109]

The death of Principal Burrows, who appears to have been universally esteemed within and without the college, occurred at the early age of 53. Yet if he still had a great deal to contribute at the time of his death, at least he was spared the furious controversy that was before long to engulf what was undoubtedly his most cherished foundation at the college, the Koraes Chair, and which was to threaten its very existence. Seton-Watson, in his obituary of Burrows, had written that there would always be a certain risk in connecting the academic and political fields. The truth of this observation was soon to be borne out.

NOTES

1. The subscribers also apparently favoured the appointment of an historian. In his letter of 30 January 1918 to the Chairman of the Board of Studies in Classics, Burrows had stressed that the subscribers were very keen that history should be the first of the three aspects of the subject. 'They mean by that to suggest that they do not wish the appointment be given to a pure philologist, but would prefer that the holder should be in the first instance a historian of Mediaeval and Modern Greece', Burrows to Platt, 30 Jan. 1918 (K).
2. Mary Gardner was the wife of Professor E.A. Gardner, Yates Professor of Archaeology at University College and formerly Director of the British School at Athens.
3. Burrows to Miller, 9 May 1918; Miller to Burrows, 20 May 1918 (K).
4. He was the author, *inter alia*, of *Cyzicus* (Cambridge, 1926) and *Christianity and Islam under the Sultans* (Oxford, 1929) 2 vols.
5. Burrows to Miller, 5 June 1918; Miller to Burrows, 11 June 1918 (K).
6. Burrows to Petrocochino, 13 July 1918 (K).
7. Burrows to Psicharis, 29 Aug. 1918 (K).
8. Burrows to A.J.B. Wace, 20 Sept. 1918 (K).
9. Burrows to Psicharis, Diehl and Pernot, 24 July 1918 (K).
10. Burrows to Eumorfopoulos, 30 May 1918; Eumorfopoulos to Burrows, 31 May 1918 (K). Both of these journalists were 'anti-Gennadius'.
11. Burrows to Petrocochino, 25 June 1918; Basdekas to Burrows, 31 Aug. 1918 (K).
12. Andreades to Burrows, 27 June 1918 (K).
13. Wace to Burrows, 9 Aug. 1918 (K).
14. *Les Etudes Franco-Grecques* was a monthly journal published in Paris between 1918 and 1921 with a subsidy from the Greek legation. Burrows was among its patrons: Dimitri

Kitsikis, *Propagande et pressions en politique internationale. La Grèce et ses revendications à la Conférence de la Paix (1919–1920)* (Paris, 1963), p. 233.

15. Maccas to Burrows, 28 July 1918 (K).
16. Drakoulis was one of the pioneers of socialism in Greece and had been elected as the first socialist deputy to the Greek Parliament in 1910. An enthusiastic supporter of the Entente, he was also a 'maximalist' in his attitude to Greece's irredentist claims.
17. Drakoulis to Burrows, 19 Aug. 1918 (K).
18. Petrides to Burrows, 4 Sept. 1918; Pernot to Burrows, 13 Sept. 1918 (K).
19. Oeconomos to Burrows, 2 Sept. 1918 (K).
20. This was published in Paris in 1918.
21. Diehl to Burrows, 11 Aug. 1918; Psicharis to Burrows, 3 Aug. 1918; Drakoulis to Burrows, 10 Aug. 1918 (K).
22. Cassavetti to Burrows, 29 Aug. 1918 (K). Ioannis Vilaras, a champion of the vernacular, published his *I romeiki glosa* in Corfu in 1814.
23. See *Report of the Committee of the Delegacy appointed with full powers to fill the vacant Lectureship in the Department of Byzantine and Modern Greek*, enclosed with Burrows' letter of 5 December 1918 to Walters.
24. *Concerning the Wars of the Balkan Allies, 1912–1913* (London, 1913).
25. *Report of the Committee of the Delegacy.*
26. Burrows to Cassavetti, 30 Sept. 1918; Oeconomos to Burrows, 30 Sept. 1918 (K). Oeconomos' main obligation was to teach Modern Greek but he was to describe himself as 'Lecturer in Modern Greek and Byzantine History at the University of London, King's College'.
27. 'Though on this particular Committee I am expert as well as Principal, I should like you and Lord Hambledon to have the chance of seeing the evidence, so that you can sign the report with good conscience. As the candidates are most of them foreigners and one of the unsuccessful ones [i.e. Christos Kessary] has done temporary work at King's, it is as well that everything should be in order', Burrows to Walters, 5 Dec. 1918.
28. C.A. Hutton to Burrows, 31 May 1918; 22 Aug. 1918 (K).
29. Toynbee to Burrows, 26 July 1918; Burrows to Toynbee 30 July 1918; Toynbee to Burrows, 22 Sept. 1918; Burrows to Toynbee, 24 Sept. 1918; Toynbee to Burrows, 25 Sept. 1918 (K)(T).
30. A tutor at Jackson's college, Queen's, and subsequently Corpus Christi Professor of Latin.
31. He was also awarded the Craven scholarship in 1903. He was an undergraduate at Queen's College between 1899 and 1903.
32. Herbert Warren to Burrows 7, 8, 19 Oct. 1918 (K). Dr David Norbrook, the Librarian of Magdalen College, Oxford, has kindly informed me that the college records show no more than that Jackson was elected to a fellowship on 21 October 1903, but the election was not confirmed following the customary year of probation. W.D. Macray in his *A Register of the Members of St Mary Magdalen College, Oxford* (Oxford, 1894–1911), vii. p. 87, stated that he 'vacated his fellowship at the end of the year of probation'. His name was not included in the 1909, 1911 and 1922 editions of the *Magdalen College Record* but he was 'rehabilitated' in the fourth edition, that of 1934: letter of 20 January 1984. Jackson's major published work was the *Marginalia Scaenica*, edited posthumously by Eduard Fraenkel (London 1955) in the series Oxford Classical and Philosophical Monographs. He also translated a number of classical texts for Oxford University Press. Fraenkel, who met Jackson shortly before he died in 1952, records that his scholarly work was carried on in the evenings after days spent working on his mother's Caldbeck farm. He considered him to have a genius for textual criticism, whose work imparted the feeling 'of being all the time in the company of a great scholar and good and lovable man'.
33. London, 1914. *Nomads of the Balkans* remains one of the most important studies of the Vlachs of the Pindus mountains.
34. Dawkins was the author of *Modern Greek in Asia Minor: A study of the dialects of Silli, Cappadocia and Pharasa with grammar, texts, translations and glossary* (Cambridge, 1916).
35. Burrows had written to Hasluck on 24 August to ask whether there were any chance of the doctors giving him a clean bill of health for he had little doubt, 'though this of course is my

own opinion', that if he were well he would be the second choice. Burrows to Hasluck, 24 Aug. 1918 (K).

36. Wace to Burrows, 9 Aug. 1918; Burrows to Wace, 20 Sept. 1918; Wace to Burrows, 7, 13 Oct. 1918 (K).
37. Dawkins to Burrows, 2 Aug. 1918; 2 Oct. 1918 (K).
38. Alan Leeper to Burrows, 24 Oct. 1918 (K).
39. Burrows to Scutt, 8 Oct. 1918; Scutt to Burrows, 10 Oct. 1918; Fisher to Burrows, 14 Oct. 1918 (K).
40. Now Heybeliadasi, one of the Princes' Islands in the sea of Marmara.
41. Blackie's substantial collection of Modern Greek books is preserved in Edinburgh University Library.
42. For an account of his experiences see *Tales of Aegean Intrigue* (London, 1920).
43. (Cambridge, 1910), p.x.
44. Presumably Sir John Stavridi.
45. *Les cinq livres de la Loi (Le Pentateuque): Traduction en néo-grec publiée en caractères hébraïques à Constantinople en 1547 ...*, (Leiden, Leipzig 1897).
46. There never in fact seems to have been a Chair of Hebrew at the University of Athens. Belleli also wrote a letter to Dimitrios Caclamanos, who had succeeded Gennadius as Greek minister in London in November 1918, blackguarding his rivals. He claimed, for instance, that Hasluck's book on *Cyzicus* had no real scientific value, while H. Idris Bell was not worth much: Kitsikis, op.cit., p.456.
47. Burrows to Seton-Watson, 15 Oct. 1918 (K). The applications of the various candidates are included with the material prepared for circulation to the members of the Board of Advisors.
48. Scutt to Burrows, 26 Nov. 1918; 3 Dec. 1918; Burrows to Scutt, 28 Nov. 1918 (K).
49. Burrows to Belleli, 26 Nov. 1918 (K).
50. Mavrogordato was to write articles on Modern Greek history for the *Encyclopaedia Britannica* and in 1931 published *Modern Greece: a Chronicle and a Survey 1800–1931* (London). At this time Mavrogordato was in receipt of a monthly stipend of £50 from the Greek Embassy for his services on behalf of the Greek cause as honorary secretary of the Anglo-Hellenic League, Kitsikis, op.cit., p.460.
51. Oeconomos apparently had an audience of 100 at these lectures: Burrows to Toynbee, 24 March 1919 (T).
52. Kitsikis, op.cit., pp.455–6.
53. Burrows to Warren, 25 Oct. 1918; Warren to Burrows, 26 Oct. 1918 (K).
54. Letter to Burrows, 11 Nov. 1918 (K).
55. Jackson to Burrows, 30 Jan. 1919, enclosed with the papers circulated for the meeting of the Board of Advisors on 24 March 1919 (S–W).
56. Eumorfopoulos, in a letter of 10 March 1918 to John Mavrogordato, had described Gennadius as behaving like a 'perfect boor' at one of the meetings of the Subscribers' Committee. 'When people talked about Gennadius being capable of such outbursts, I always thought they exaggerated; that there was some cause for his behaviour. I know better now.' (K)
57. Burrows to Pember Reeves, 29 Jan. 1919; Burrows to Macmillan, 2 Feb. 1919. At least one member of the Board of Advisors, however, Sir F.C. Kenyon, would have been prepared to support Gennadius' candidature had Burrows seen fit: Kenyon to Burrows, 28 Jan. 1919 (K).
58. Burrows to Khatzidakis, 12 Feb. 1919; Khatzidakis to Burrows, 15 March 1919 (K).
59. On Venizelos' memorandum, see Michael Llewellyn-Smith, *Ionian Vision. The Greek Campaign in Asia Minor* (London 1973), pp.71–4. The following week Burrows was among the speakers at a meeting held under the auspices of The Committee for the Redemption of Saint Sophia. The Committee argued that there could be no peace in Europe until Saint Sophia had been redeemed and that 'there can be no peace of mind to British Christians until the last remaining sign of the disgrace of a century's support of the Turk is blotted out', *Give back ... Saint Sophia* (London 1919). It is difficult to quantify the practical effect of Burrows' unflagging championship of the Greek cause. But the British High Commissioner in Constantinople, Admiral Sir John de Robeck, paid him the oblique compliment of wondering whether the harshness of the peace terms imposed on

the Turks might in part be due to 'the thunder of the Canons of Canterbury, to the outcry of Near Eastern cranks, and to the ingenious enthusiasm of Dr Burrows and his friends', *Documents on British Foreign Policy 1919–1939*, 1st series, Vol. xiii (London, 1963), p. 19.

60. Toynbee at this time evidently shared in the general admiration for Venizelos that was the fashion at the Peace Conference. On 5 March 1919, for instance, he wrote to Burrows that Venizelos had 'evidently made an extraordinary personal impression on the Conference. I don't wonder. The Greeks are lucky to have him ...' (K). Cf Harold Nicolson, *Peace-making* (London 1933), p. 136.

61. Burrows to Toynbee, 15 Jan. 1919; Toynbee to Burrows, 21 Jan. 1919; Toynbee to Burrows, 28 Jan. 1919 (T)(K).

62. Rumours were circulating among the Greek community that Zaharoff was prepared to offer £1,000,000 for a Greek university in Constantinople, Eumorfopoulos to Burrows, 16 Feb. 1919 (K). No such university was founded but a Greek university was established in Smyrna during the period of Greek administration between 1919 and 1922. On this see Victoria Solomonidis, 'Greece in Asia Minor: The Greek administration of the Vilayet of Aidin, 1919–1922', University of London PhD thesis 1985, pp. 183ff.

63. This was the Committee for the Redemption of Saint Sophia of which Canon J.A. Douglas, later a staunch opponent of Toynbee in the Senate of the University of London, was an honorary secretary.

64. Murray to Burrows, 3 Feb. 1919; Burrows to Murray, 4 Feb. 1919 (K).

65. Arnold Toynbee, the socialist thinker after whom Toynbee Hall in Whitechapel was named.

66. Murray to Burrows, 4 Feb. 1919; Headlam-Morley to Burrows, 27 Jan. 1919; Smith to Burrows, 2 Feb. 1919; Rendall to Burrows, 7 Feb. 1919; Wace to Burrows, 15 Feb. 1919 (S–W).

67. He had been rejected as unfit as a result of contracting dysentery from drinking bad water while on a long hike from Kato Vezani to Gythion on 26 April 1912: A.J. Toynbee, *A Study of History* (Oxford 1954), x, pp. 236–7.

68. *Journal of Hellenic Studies*, xxxii (1913), pp. 246–75.

69. London 1914.

70. By Neville Forbes, Arnold J. Toynbee, D. Mitrany and D.G. Hogarth, Oxford, 1916.

71. London, 1915.

72. London, 1915.

73. Documents presented to Viscount Grey of Fallodon by Viscount Bryce, London HMSO, 1916. Cd. 8325. Miscellaneous No. 31.

74. *Curriculum vitae* circulated in mid-March by Deller to the Board of Advisors for the Chair (S–W).

75. 'The topography of Boeotia and the theories of M. Bérard' and 'The literary evidence for the topography of Thebes', *Annual of the British School at Athens*, xvii (1910–11), pp. 29–53; xviii (1911–12), pp. 189–210.

76. *Journal of Hellenic Studies*, xxxiii (1913), pp. 53–72, 223–45.

77. Myres to the Secretary to the Academic Registrar, 11 March 1919 (S–W).

78. Burrows to Myres, 18 March 1919; Myres to Burrows, 19 March 1919 (K).

79. On his copy of this letter Toynbee subsequently pencilled a note to the effect that Burrows had made no mention of a committee of subscribers having any say in his programme.

80. Toynbee to Burrows, 24 March 1919; Burrows to Toynbee, 24 March 1919; Burrows to Toynbee, 25 March 1919; Toynbee to Burrows, 27 March 1919 (Y)(K).

81. Burrows to Gomme, 25 March 1919 (K).

82. Nicolson, op.cit., p. 312.

83. Toynbee to Burrows, 17 April 1919; Burrows to Toynbee, 19 April 1919; Toynbee to Burrows, 22 April 1919; Burrows to Toynbee, 25 April 1919 (K). A copy of Burrows' letter of 25 April, in Toynbee's hand, is also to be found in the Seton-Watson papers.

84. The Academic Registrar to Toynbee, 29 May 1919 (T).

85. Toynbee to Burrows, 27 May 1919; Burrows to Toynbee, 28 May 1919; Rosalind Toynbee to Burrows, 2 June 1919; Burrows to Rosalind Toynbee, 5 June 1919 (K).

86. This appears not to have been published.

87. Toynbee to Seton-Watson, 17 July 1919, 8 Aug. 1919 (S–W).

88. Toynbee replied on 22 May that his feelings about Smyrna were tempered by the fact that the Italians had occupied a large slice in the south and south-west of Anatolia. He feared that although Greece might be able to secure the immediate zone around Smyrna 'the wider hinterland in Anatolia which might otherwise have been given to Hellenism will be· closed to it by Italian policing'. He believed that in the natural course of events Anatolia would have eventually become 'a Greek and Armenian country in the west and east respectively, and that the Moslems would gradually have disappeared'. It was, he believed, fairly clear, as it had turned out, that Smyrna could only fall to Greece through a general partition of Anatolia 'and I believe this will be less advantageous to Greece in the long run than the more gradual solution': Toynbee to Burrows 22 May 1919 (K).

89. On the diplomatic background to the Greek landing see Llewellyn-Smith, op.cit., pp. 62–85. On the incidents following the landing see Solomonidis, op.cit., pp. 58ff. These gave rise to an inter-allied commission of inquiry whose findings were highly critical of the Greek army of occupation. The report of this Commission Interalliée d'Enquête sur l'Occupation grecque de Smyrna et des Territoires adjacents is published in *Documents on British Foreign Policy 1919–1939*, 1st series, Vol. ii (London, 1948), pp. 237–58.

90. Burrows to Venizelos, 21 and 28 June 1919. Venizelos draft reply in Greek (undated), Venizelos Archive file 314, Benaki Museum, Athens. I am grateful to Dr George Mavrogordatos for drawing my attention to this correspondence. Burrows' letter of 28 June and Venizelos' reply of 9 July are printed in Glasgow, op.cit., pp. 264–5, 256–62.

91. Glasgow, op.cit., p. 269. At the same time Pember Reeves was made a Knight Grand Commander of the Order of George I, while Mavrogordato and Harold Spender, another prominent member of the Anglo-Hellenic League, were made Knight Companions of the Gold Cross of the Order of the Redeemer. Eumorfopoulos was made a Knight Companion of the Gold Cross of the Order of George I. Burrows had already been made a Commander of the Royal Order of the Saviour in 1914.

92. Horace Rumbold, *Final Recollections of a Diplomatist* (London, 1905), p. 35.

93. Yannis Psicharis, whose *To taxeidi mou* (Athens, 1888) is a major landmark in the struggle to establish *dimotiki* as the literary language, taught Modern Greek in Paris and, as we have seen, had been in correspondence with Burrows over the chair. A subsequent holder of the chair in his own inaugural lecture misread Gennadius' strictures as applying to Psicharis and his concert of *socialist* youths, Cyril Mango, 'Byzantinism and Romantic Hellenism', *Journal of the Warburg and Courtauld Institutes*, xxviii (1965), p. 29. An understandable misreading although it is characteristic of Gennadius to have used such an arcane epithet.

94. Toynbee to Burrows, 23 Oct. 1919 (K).

95. *The Place of Mediaeval and Modern Greece in History* (London, 1919).

96. Toynbee to Burrows, 23 Oct. 1919; Eumorfopoulos to Burrows, 9 Oct. 1919 (K).

97. Kitsikis, op.cit., p. 457.

98. Glasgow, op.cit., p. 280.

99. Ibid., pp. xii–xiii.

100. At the San Remo conference the terms of the Treaty of Sèvres which, in theory, constituted the peace settlement liquidating the Ottoman Empire, were agreed. The treaty, which was signed on 10 August, was highly favourable to Greece but was never ratified by the Turkish nationalists who repudiated the acceptance of the treaty by the supine government of the Sultan in Constantinople. After five years the Smyrna region, following either a plebiscite or a vote in a local parliament, could be annexed by Greece. At the same time Greek sovereignty was recognized over the Aegean islands with the exception of Rhodes, while Greece was awarded almost the whole of Thrace. Truly Venizelos' supporters could proclaim that he had created a Greece of 'the two continents and of the five seas'. But the triumph was to prove hollow and short-lived and already there were indications that the Greek position in Asia Minor was becoming untenable and that there was no hope of enforcing the settlement by force of arms.

101. Burrows, like most observers, Toynbee included, clearly expected Venizelos to be swept back to power in the elections scheduled for November 1920. He assumed that the electorate would be eternally grateful to a Venizelos, whose adroit diplomacy and the almost hypnotic fascination he had exercised over the luminaries gathered at the Paris peace conference had secured for Greece a settlement incorporating most of its irredentist

demands. In fact, however, Venizelos was to suffer a crushing defeat and was to retreat forthwith to a self-imposed exile in France. The reasons for his defeat are complex. One powerful factor was undoubtedly the extent to which he had become associated in the minds of many Greeks with the repeated and flagrant infringements of Greek sovereignty committed by the Entente Powers during the First World War.

102. Venizelos Archive, Benaki Museum, file no. 267.
103. In his draft of this message Venizelos had included 'Greeks' at this point but subsequently deleted it.
104. Venizelos Archive Benaki Museum, file no. 267. The text of the telegram which Venizelos sent to Mrs Burrows on hearing of Burrows' death is to be found in Glasgow, op.cit., p. 294, the original draft in the Venizelos Archive, file no. 267.
105. *The New Europe*, 20 May 1919, quoted in Hugh and Christopher Seton-Watson, op.cit., pp. 403–4.
106. Glasgow, op.cit., p. 294.
107. University of London, Senate Minutes, 1920, 3966.
108. I am kindly informed by Sodos Georgallis of the Cyprus High Commission in London that the street continues to be named after Principal Burrows.
109. An appeal, under distinguished patronage, to endow the Burrows library was launched to coincide with the college's centenary in 1928. Among the most generous gifts was a superb collection of several hundred volumes donated by William Miller and the library of Alexander Pallis, the Liverpudlian demoticist. Burrows' own library formed its nucleus.

3. The Controversy

During the first year of his tenure of the Koraes Chair Toynbee was engaged in planning his courses and in creating the nucleus of a departmental library, activities which brought him into frequent contact with Gennadius' successor as the Greek minister in London, Dimitrios Caclamanos, to whom he apparently turned for advice on the structuring of his courses in history and how best to confront the thorny problem of the language question.[1] For Yannis Psicharis in Paris, one of the leading protagonists of the demotic, had inevitably been infuriated by Gennadius' injunction to the Koraes professor that the new department should eschew the vulgar demotic. Psicharis exhorted Toynbee to take a clear position on the language question by condemning the 'purified' *katharevousa*. Toynbee prudently replied that although personally in favour of the demotic he could not take a public position in a debate between Greek scholars, for he himself was not Greek, a stand in which he was supported by John Mavrogordato.[2] Toynbee, however, was undoubtedly not over-burdened with teaching in a post which was clearly going to be very much what he chose to make of it. In the summer of 1920 he applied for study leave, hoping, as he wrote to Seton-Watson in September 1920, to get out to Greece to see 'how Greece is handling her Moslem minority' in the new provinces.[3] On 20 October he was granted by the Senate of the University two terms leave of absence to travel to Greece, there to establish connections 'with Professors, officials and publishers in order to strengthen the bonds between Greece and the Department of Modern Greek in the College'.[4] No reference was made to the fact that Toynbee, during his visit to the Greek lands, was to act as a special correspondent of the *Manchester Guardian*.

Toynbee arrived in Athens in mid-January 1921, a few weeks after Venizelos' defeat in the elections of November 1920 which in turn had led to the restoration of King Constantine I to the throne from which he had been banished by the Entente Allies in 1917. These developments had taken Toynbee as much by surprise as almost all other observers. At the end of January he travelled to Smyrna. For his main interest had always been to establish how well Greece was coping with the mandate entrusted by the Allies of administering an ethnically mixed population, one constituent in which was composed of Greeks. During the next two months he made three journeys into the hinterland to see how the Greek administration was faring in practice. In the first of these, between 1 and 8 February, he visited Alaşehir, Uşak, Kula, Salıhlı and Sardis (Sart); in the second Ephesus (Efes), Kirkince, Aydın, Tire and Torbalı. While visiting Ephesus, Toynbee was subject to one of the mystical experiences that occurred at different periods in his life. This was to prove the most vivid of his several 'experiences of the local annihilation of Time in places where Time had stood still'. Approaching the theatre from a hill above the ancient city on 11 February:

> At the instant at which this historic panorama impinged on the spectator's eyes, the empty theatre peopled itself with a tumultuous

throng as the breath came into the dead and they lived and stood upon their feet ... These two dishevelled figures must be Gaius and Aristarchus; that ineffectual-looking creature must be Alexander. What is this rhythmic roar into which the babel of tongues is resolving itself? Will Gaius and Aristarchus escape with their lives? Thank Heaven for the intrepid town clerk's promptness and presence of mind. But at the moment when the cries of 'Great is Diana' are dying down and the clerk is beginning to reason tactfully with the crowd, the life flickers out of the scene as the spectator is carried up again instantaneously to the current surface of the Time-stream from an abyss, nineteen centuries deep into which the impact of the sight of the theatre at Ephesus had plunged him.[5]

Toynbee's third excursion in Western Asia Minor, between 26 February and 10 March, took in Manısa (Magnesia), Soma, Kinik, Bergama (Pergamum), Ayvalık and Dikeli.

Naturally the Greek authorities in Asia Minor took a close interest in his travels, and in particular in his contacts with the Turkish population in the occupied territories, and they were understandably anxious that Toynbee should form as favourable an impression as possible of the nature of the Greek administration. Dimitrios Rallis, the Prime Minister, on 8 January 1921, telegraphed the Greek High Commission to assist Toynbee in carrying out his mission for this would serve Greece's national interests. The High Commissioner in turn instructed his subordinates to try to ensure that the Turks in their territory wholeheartedly expressed their gratitude towards the Greek administration for its impartiality and the security which it afforded. The Greeks were to be encouraged to demonstrate sentiments of friendship and gratitude towards England and their determination to make any sacrifice to preserve their newly-won emancipation. He also authorised the payment of expenses incurred in respect of Toynbee's visits. For his visit to Soma these amounted to 3,762 grosia. Aristeides Stergiadis' subordinates duly did what was expected of them and some of their reports are preserved in archives of the Greek Ministry of Foreign Affairs. There is a clear element of wishful thinking in these, although it should be borne in mind that they all relate to Toynbee's travels before he was a witness to atrocities committed by the Greek army in the Yalova region in May.

The gendarmerie in Manısa, for instance, reported that, at a discussion of Greece's national claims and rights with local Greek notables, Toynbee had 'unreservedly expressed his philhellenic sentiments'. At the house of one Veziroğlu, a Turk was reported to have told Toynbee that in no circumstances would they accept the Greek administration. At the same time he had criticized harshly the former administration of the Committee of Union and Progress. In the course of a visit to a Greek school in the town Toynbee is reported to have expressed his admiration for 'Greek progress'. In conversation with a gendarmerie officer Toynbee is reported to have expatiated on the justice of the Greek cause and to have blackened the Italians and French, calling them propagandists. He hoped that within a short time the command to advance would be given to the Greek army, a move which he was confident would result in the rout of Mustafa Kemal. To a group of Greeks assembled in the house of one Kamberopoulos he is alleged to have stated that he would defend Greek rights to the best of his ability, for England and Greece were bound by common interests. The Muslim prefect of Manısa, Husni Tzevi Zaade, assured him that if the Greek administration had not vouchsafed justice and equality he would not have remained *en poste*. He also detailed to Toynbee the dastardly acts of the 'Kemalist hordes' and of the Committee of Union and Progress against the Greeks. The prefect emphasized that if the former Turkish administration were to be restored then he, together with three-quarters of the Turkish element in the population, would move elsewhere. At a lunch it was stressed that whereas Greece had always been indebted to England, it was now infinitely indebted for Greece had been established 'as the vanguard of civilization in the East under the sceptre of England'. Toynbee was observed filling his notebook with 'philhellenic notes'.[6]

During his travels in Western Asia Toynbee was certainly very conscious of the bloodshed that had accompanied the Greek landings in mid-May 1919 and the Turkish reprisals and Greek counter-reprisals that had ensued in the region of Aydin, together with the policy of deportations practised by both sides. He believed these had, however, only become organized on the Greek side in the wake of the battle of Inönü in late March/early April 1921 and it was only after he had moved in mid-March from Smyrna to Constantinople, from where he made a number of forays into Greek-controlled regions on the southern shores of the Sea of Marmara and, in particular, to the Yalova-Gemlik peninsula, that he was confronted by first-hand evidence of Greek atrocities. Towards the end of his life he recalled how, having looked at the Greek-Turkish war from the Greek side of the front, faithful to the precept *Audi alteram partem*, he had sought to get an insight into the conflict from the Turkish side. Here he had run up against a barrier of hostility and suspicion, for it was known that he had worked for Lord Bryce in compiling the Blue Book on Turkish treatment of the Armenians and, to the Turks, Bryce was almost as bad a name as Gladstone. He was, moreover, a professor of Modern Greek studies, and was the representative of that most Gladstonian of British newspapers, the *Manchester Guardian*.

Toynbee recalled that, after a number of unprofitable interviews with Hamid Bey, the director of the Red Crescent in Constantinople, he was challenged at short notice to board a Red Crescent ship, the *Gül-i Nihal*, sailing to Yalova with a representative of the Allied High Commissioners in Constantinople on board. On returning to the capital Toynbee showed Hamid Bey the text of the telegram, reporting on the atrocities that he had witnessed, that he had sent to the *Manchester Guardian*. Hamid Bey had been highly surprised by Toynbee's display of even-handedness and was even more surprised to receive a few days later, a copy of the paper in which Toynbee's dispatch had been printed. He recalled that, after almost 50 years, he could still see the scene in the Red Crescent offices: 'big Hamid Bey with the English newspaper in his hands, and his colleagues crowding round, with radiant faces. Their case was being put in Britain at last'.[7] During these travels in the Marmara region Toynbee, accompanied by his wife, put together an extensive dossier detailing Greek atrocities in the area. At the same time he sent back numerous dispatches to the *Manchester Guardian* repeating his strictures against the Greek army of occupation. On 27 May, for instance, Toynbee reported that in the Yalova district

> the whole Moslem population is terrorised and in daily danger of death ... These events are part of a general extermination of the Moslems in the Karamursal peninsula. The malignity and inhumanity of the local Greek military authorities are undisguised ... If Greece values her status as a civilised nation her government must stop the atrocities, dismiss the officers implicated, and facilitate the alleviation of the pitiable condition of the victims. Meanwhile, instant action by the Allied Governments and pressure of public opinion are essential.[8]

Although the only atrocities to which he had actually been a witness were committed by Greeks he made no effort to play down the fact that similar outrages had been committed on the Turkish side. But it would, he was to argue in *The Western Question in Greece and Turkey*, which he was to write at great speed on his return from the Near East, be a gross error of judgement to assume that the Turks were more unrighteous than the Greeks. If it were true, as it was, that the Turks had committed more atrocities against the Greeks than *vice versa* this was only because the Turks had had more opportunities for such wrong-doing. For between 1461 and 1821 there had been very few Greeks who had not been under Turkish rule, while Greeks had only had considerable numbers of Turks in their power since 1912. To anyone inclined to believe that there was much to choose between the Greek and Turkish record in respect of atrocities he recommended a somewhat bizarre calculation whereby the total number of atrocities inflicted by Greeks and Turks on each other should be divided by the number of opportunities to inflict them, with the result being weighted ('if the evidence suffices') by the strength of the stimulus in each particular case.[9]

The Supreme Council, as Toynbee was to write in *The Western Question*, had set the Greeks the most difficult administrative task conceivable, namely that 'of governing a country with a mixed population in which one of the elements was of the same nationality as themselves'. Just as 'the problem of ruling Turks and non-Turks in the Ottoman Empire had completely beaten the Osmanlis', so the Greeks had proved incapable of supporting 'the Osmanli's "burden"'. It was his considered judgement that good administration in Anatolia under the Greeks was no more possible than it had been in Macedonia after 1878 under the Turks. He believed, moreover, that, as the conflict had continued, so the quality of the Turkish administration had improved, while that of the Greek had declined. He argued that by September 1921 a solution to the conflict could come about only through foreign intervention or through the exhaustion of one of the parties, and he believed it more probable that the Greeks would crack first. He predicted, correctly, that a radical segregation of the communities would be the most likely outcome of the conflict. While critical of the 'imperious personality of Mr Venizelos' who had pushed Greece into a policy of 'reckless aggrandisement', he also had harsh words for Britain and France who had launched Greece into its hopeless Anatolian entanglement. Moreover, if the Greek landings at Smyrna had acted as the catalyst for the Turkish national movement, then British support for the Sultan's government in Constantinople had made its fortune. Greece had been employed by the Western powers as their principal Near Eastern pawn and had proved 'as incapable as Turkey (or for that matter any Western country) of governing well a mixed population containing an alien majority and a minority of her own nationality'.[10] Moreover, Toynbee, in addition to his journalistic and other writings on the Greek–Turkish imbroglio,[11] took a more active role in actually trying to shape the course of events, although this was presumably not publicly known at the time. In July 1921, for instance, he sent Forbes Adam of the Foreign Office a summary of a three-hour discussion between himself and Rauf Ahmet Bey, who had accompanied Bekir Sami Bey to the London Conference of February–March of that year at which a solution to the crisis had been unsuccessfully sought. Lord Curzon mentioned the indication of Kemalist terms contained in Toynbee's paper in his own memorandum 'respecting intervention between Greece and Turkey' and composed in October 1921. Apparently unaware of Toynbee's academic status, he referred to him as 'the correspondent of the *Manchester Guardian*, who has transferred his sympathies from the Greeks to the Turks'.[12]

Toynbee had, of course, anticipated the controversy that his reporting of the Anatolian crisis was likely to provoke and had first offered to place his resignation in the hands of Principal Barker, Burrows' successor, in May 1921, writing by the same post by which he had sent his first dispatches to the *Manchester Guardian* reporting on the commission of atrocities by the Greek army of occupation.[13] He repeated this offer a year later, writing to Barker on 6 May 1922 that 'if ever circumstances (of which one is rather at the mercy in these cases, and of which one can never quite foresee the ramifications) should make it desirable, in the interests of the College and the University, that I should at any time offer my resignation, I should do that at once, and, in fact, should be grateful for a hint from you at the earliest moment that you felt that it should be done'. He sincerely hoped, however, that such a possibility was remote, for resignation would constitute 'a considerable disaster for me'. In the same letter he thanked Barker for his suggested alterations to the preface of the *Western Question in Greece and Turkey*, some of which he accepted, some he rejected. He told Barker that he quite saw the importance of not letting it appear as if he had been given leave of absence by the university so as especially to study the political crisis. Of course, he added, 'when I first broached the question of leave of absence with you in August 1920, I thought that Venizelos would endure for ever, and I also never expected to witness Greek atrocities'. He had also expected that the crisis would have been rapidly resolved by the evacuation of Anatolia but the London conference of February–March 1921 had come to nothing. What he had done, 'most idiotically', in the draft preface had been to project his current state of mind into his attitude at the time he applied to the university for leave of absence 'a mistake which would have laid both the

University and me open to possible criticisms which we neither of us deserve'.[14]

In this revised preface, dated 22 March 1922, Toynbee clearly anticipated an unfavourable reaction to a book one of whose basic conclusions was that the Greeks had demonstrated 'the same unfitness as the Turks for governing a mixed population'. He submitted that he was not to be convicted of partiality 'by the fact that, in discussing particular chapters of a long story, I sum up against one party in favour of the other'. The fact that he was neither a Greek nor a Turk, he maintained, created little presumption of his being fair-minded 'for Western partisans of non-Western peoples are often more fanatical than their favourites'. It might, he wrote, be 'painful to Greeks and "Philhellenes" that information and reflections unfavourable to Greece should have been published by the first occupant of the Korais Chair'. He regretted this, but 'from an academic point of view' it was less unfortunate than if his conclusions on the Anatolian entanglement had been favourable to Greece and unfavourable to Turkey.

> The actual circumstances, whatever personal unpleasantness they may entail for me and my Greek friends and acquaintances, at least preclude the suspicion that an endowment of learning in a British University has been used for propaganda on behalf of the country with which it is concerned. Such a contention, if it could be urged, would be serious; for academic study should have no political purpose, although, when its subject is history, its judgements upon the nature and causal connection of past events do occasionally and incidentally have some effect upon the present and the future.

In conclusion he explained how it came about that the groundwork for the book had been undertaken while he was acting as a special correspondent of the *Manchester Guardian*. The newspaper had not only paid his expenses but had conferred on him the status which those like himself who were 'not persons of eminence' needed in order to meet 'important people' and to witness 'important events'.[15]

The book duly appeared in the early summer of 1922, a few months before the catastrophic defeat of the Greek armies in Asia Minor, the subsequent burning of Smyrna and the uprooting, in the ensuing Exchange of Populations, of Greek communities, some of which had been established for thousands of years. The book's topicality ensured that it was widely, and promptly, reviewed. Many of the reviews[16] were favourable and acquitted the author of the charge of partiality. Inevitably, however, the book, coinciding as it did with a disaster without parallel in recent Greek history, attracted fierce criticism in Greek circles. One such onslaught, by Major G. Melas, of the Devonshire Club and formerly secretary to ex-king Constantine, was entitled *The Turk as he is: Answer to a libel: Sidelights on ... Kemalism, Bolshevism and Pan-Germanism*.[17] This was a swingeing attack on Toynbee and his 'unsatiated hatred for the Greeks', complete with the insinuation that this 'blind disciple of Fallmerayer' had been bought. Expatiating on the nomadic ancestry of the Turks, Major Melas asked whether

Toynbee knew many Turks who would close the door behind them. 'Small facts sometimes prove much.'[18]

One indirect but obvious riposte to Toynbee was compiled by a member of his own department, Lysimachos Oeconomos. After the burning of Smyrna in mid-September, he rapidly put together a collection of press reports and eye-witness accounts of Turkish atrocities which was already in print by the end of the year. This was *The Martyrdom of Smyrna and Eastern Christendom: a file of overwhelming evidence, denouncing the misdeeds of the Turks in Asia Minor and showing their responsibility for the horrors of Smyrna.*[19] Oeconomos was also the author of an Anglo-Hellenic League pamphlet, *The Tragedy of the Christian Near East*, with an appendix on *The Smyrna Holocaust* by the Rev. Charles Dobson.[20] Although on the title page of *The Martyrdom of Smyrna* Oeconomos gave his title as 'Lecturer in Modern Greek and Byzantine History at the University of London (King's College)', in his preface, dated 6 November 1922, he nowhere makes mention of Toynbee or of *The Western Question*. Oeconomos argued that 'Smyrna's *auto-de-fé*, Smyrna's sacrifice to the Mohammedan Moloch, was not only a Greek disaster, it was a European disaster, a disaster for civilization'.[21] Oeconomos' appointment in the department expired at the end of December 1922. He voluntarily continued teaching until February 1923, when he was replaced for the teaching of Modern Greek by K. Kyriakides, a Cypriot attached to the Greek Legation.[22]

The Western Question (which had also been published by Houghton, Mifflin in New York) rapidly went into a second edition, which appeared early in 1923, and to which Toynbee appended a preface, dated 20 November 1922, adverting to the extent to which his earlier analysis had been confirmed by events, and bringing the story up to date to the extent that this had proved necessary. He pointed out that, despite all his efforts while travelling in the disputed territories and on his return home and despite the warnings of their representatives on the spot, Western statesmen had failed to act to prevent a disaster which to him had appeared obvious and inevitable unless and until their policies had been modified. During his travels he had acquired an affection not only for Smyrna but also for Manisa, Bergama, Ayvalık and many other smaller places, where he had made friends with people 'of almost every denomination and nationality'. 'These beautiful towns are now desolated, these amiable people killed, exiled, ruined, or tormented by the most appalling mental and physical agonies, and this through the wantonness of Western statesmen who hardened their hearts and stopped their ears against their own expert advisers.' Besides sorrow for the victims he felt indignation 'that the real criminals should have got off so cheaply. After causing hundreds of thousands of fellow human beings to lose everything that makes life worth living, they have themselves lost nothing more irretrievable than office and reputation'. He believed that his prophecy that Greek regular and irregular forces 'would eclipse their previous record of atrocities and devastations' if they withdrew after a collapse in morale had been borne out by events. He maintained, however, that if the Athens government had shown itself incapable of ruling over a Turkish majority, it was none the less indefensible to argue that the Greeks of

Cyprus were unfit to govern themselves. He bitterly criticized the Lloyd George coalition government, which had encouraged Greek claims to territories in Asia Minor with a Turkish majority, for not having carried its 'ostentatious "Philhellenism" to the length of granting self-determination to a Greek majority in a country recently annexed to the British Empire'. 'Generous in giving away what lawfully belonged to the Turks, they drew the line at surrendering what they themselves were holding with the slenderest legal title or moral right'. For very shame the British nation should redress this injustice.[23]

The first inkling of the trouble brewing for Toynbee in the college and university occurred when the Subscribers' Committee held, on 24 January 1923, what appears to have been its first meeting since the establishment of the chair. The purpose of the meeting was to discuss why the committee had never received either the annual scheme of work or the triennial report of the department's work 'with a request for criticism and suggestions', as had been asked for by the subscribers when they had made over the endowment to the university in April 1918. Those present at the meeting, Gennadius, Ionides, Marchetti and Nicholas Eumorfopoulos, resolved to write to the Secretary of King's College to complain of this omission. During the meeting it was further pointed out that the public lectures in the Department of Modern Greek advertised for the Lent term 1923 seemed to have 'only a remote connection (if any) with the Department concerned'.[24] This was a reference to six public lectures to be given by Toynbee himself on 'The Expansion of Europe Overland: The Route of the Steppes'. Two of the lectures were entitled 'The Turco-Mongol Outbreak (AD 975–1275)' and 'The Organization of the Mongol Empire'.[25] In a letter dated 26 January, Eumorfopoulos, the secretary of the Subscribers' Committee, wrote to S.J. Shovelton, the Secretary of King's College, that he had been instructed to point out that no scheme of work had yet been received nor had the first triennial report. He asked for the report, which should contain a 'list of the lectures in the department with a statement of the number of students in each session, and a list of original papers published, together with any other information dealing with the work of the Department'.[26]

The arrival of this letter was not only the first intimation that Toynbee was to receive of the conditions attaching to the chair but also the first time that Ernest Barker, who had succeeded Burrows as Principal in 1920,[27] was to learn of the conditions. For on 31 January he wrote to Toynbee that 'you can count upon me absolutely to do whatever I can to maintain the freedom of teaching – a thing I value above most things, but which seems to me to have been entirely sacrificed at the time of the foundation of the Chair which you hold. The position in which you and I consequently find ourselves is to me simply tragic'. In Barker's view the university should never have accepted the endowment on these terms ('but what is done is done'), none the less if it had accepted then indeed it had a duty to inform the holder and, indeed, the candidates. Moreover, Principal Burrows, when Toynbee had written to him in April 1919 to ask him about the rumours that had reached him of dissatisfaction with his appointment, should have explained the position fully.[28]

On being informed of the request of the Subscribers' Committee, Toynbee appears to have turned to his father-in-law, Gilbert Murray, for advice as to whether, and how, he should respond. For on 2 February Murray advised Toynbee that 'obviously it will not do to quarrel with the University ... Less obviously, perhaps, it will not do to quarrel with the Greeks unless they insist'. He should take care not to give the impression that he might be a source of trouble to other possible university employers. He recommended that Toynbee submit the report. To do so would be 'quite natural not only as a matter of courtesy from you, but as a sign of interest on the part of the Greeks'. 'Things may get to the point', he added, 'when you will have to resign rather than submit to unreasonable conditions. But I think it very important that you should show the Greeks all possible courtesy and reasonableness in the meantime'.[29] Acting in the spirit of this advice Toynbee duly and promptly sent his report to the Subscribers' Committee on 2 February via the Secretary of King's College, together with a conciliatory covering letter. In this he expressed his great regret that he had neither presented a report the previous summer nor the scheme of work due each term[30] in accordance with the undertakings apparently given by the Senate to the Committee. The reason for this was that these undertakings had never been made known, officially or unofficially, either to the Secretary of King's College or to Toynbee himself, and that the first they had heard of them was when they had received the Committee's letter earlier in the week. At this point Barker added a note to the effect that, as Principal, he had no 'cognisance whatever' of the undertakings. The Secretary of King's College, in his covering letter of 3 February, observed that the college had not been requested by the university to furnish a report and, in doing so, had undertaken no direct obligation.[31]

During the first session, 1919–1920, Toynbee had, on his own initiative, circulated termly programmes of work to the members of the Anglo-Hellenic League in order to bring the existence and activities of the chair to the notice of interested parties. But he had discontinued this practice on grounds of expense. Subsequently he had only reported to the Principal, as did other heads of department in the college. In addition to his academic work specifically connected with the chair, he was a member of the University Boards of Studies in History, Oriental Languages and Slavonic Studies; for two terms he had acted as joint secretary of the History Board, and had recently been helping out in the Classics Department during the illness of Professor Walters. He was, moreover, in accordance with the suggestion of one of the members of the Board of Advisors which had appointed him to the chair, learning Classical Arabic 'which is almost indispensable for Byzantine Studies'. Somewhat disingenuously, in view of the uproar occasioned by his various writings on the Anatolian entanglement, he wrote that, thanks to the leave of absence granted during the second and third terms of the session 1920–21, he had been able to increase his knowledge of the Greek lands 'by travelling in and around Smyrna and Constantinople, where I had never been before' and by studying on the spot Mistra, Siatista and other places of importance to medieval and modern Greek history. He concluded by stating that he would be happy to receive any criticism or suggestions regarding the report which the Committee might wish to make.

Toynbee's report was substantial, amounting to ten typewritten pages and was divided into six sections: (i) academic lectures on history, (ii) instruction in the language, (iii) public lectures, (iv) post-graduate work, (v) library and (vi) publications. During the session 1920–21 he had lectured on 'The Ottoman Empire and the Renascence of Modern Greece' to undergraduates. During the session 1921–22 he had given a course of lectures on 'The Comparative Historical Geography of Greece: Ancient, Mediaeval and Modern' in an effort to attract students taking courses in geography, history, classics and archaeology in the different colleges of the university. The result, however, had been disappointing and he had attracted only two students, both from King's College. During the current session (1922–23) he had acted as co-ordinator of a course entitled 'Outlines of Near and Middle Eastern History'. During the second and third terms of the 1919–20 session he had given a course of 20 lectures on 'Outlines of Greek History, 4th–13th centuries AD.'. During the first term of the 1921–22 session he had given a course of ten public lectures on the current situation in Greece and Turkey, arising from his experiences during his leave of absence abroad earlier in the year. (These presumably formed the basis of *The Western Question in Greece and Turkey*.) The average attendance had been about 25. In an effort to develop postgraduate work in the department he had advertised in various learned journals a project on 'Western Travellers in the Levant: 1650–1856' and had attracted a group of some eight members, including civil servants, school-mistresses and a presbyterian minister. Each member had been assigned the task of analysing different travellers' narratives and the results of their researches had been discussed at weekly seminars. Although all members of the group were part-timers he felt that the project had been well worth while. He had also put considerable effort into building up the departmental library, which he believed to be more or less unique in London, if not England. His efforts to develop the library further had been hampered by the failure of the Greek government to pay its annual sub-vention, some £50 of which had been earmarked for the library.[32] In the same report he gave details of Dr Oeconomos' activities in teaching Greek during the 1921–22 session. Such little demand for classes in Modern Greek as existed had come from archaeologists, travellers and people with some family connection with Greece. He believed that Modern Greek would be studied in London 'in a dilettante and desultory way' but would not be taken up as a commercial language. He added that Oeconomos was in no way to blame for the slender results so far achieved. Oeconomos had, in addition, given a course of five public lectures on the political career of Ioannis Capodistrias, the first president of Greece, based on original research in the French and British archives.[33]

Toynbee's report of 2 February was placed before the next meeting of the Subscribers' Committee, held on 20 February and attended by Gennadius, Ionides, Marchetti and Eumorfopoulos. After lengthy discussion it was decided to adjourn the meeting to a later date and to invite William Pember Reeves, the Director of the London School of Economics and a prominent member of the Anglo-Hellenic League, to be present. This adjourned meeting, attended by Gennadius, Ionides and Eumorfopoulos, took place on 9 March but without Pember Reeves who had informed Gennadius that for various reasons he considered it inadvisable to attend. On 26 February, however, Pember Reeves had written to Eumorfopoulos (on Anglo-Hellenic League notepaper) commenting on Toynbee's report. Although not actively involved in the establishment of the Koraes Chair, Pember Reeves had hoped that it would prove successful: 'No honest Philhellene could have wished otherwise'. He considered the work of the department to have been very meagre. During Toynbee's second year he had given only ten lectures before leaving for his two terms' leave of absence in the Near East, 'where, though he does not mention it, he engaged in newspaper work of a political and controversial kind'. Over four years he had given 67 lectures, an annual average of 17, which was 'extremely little' when compared with the workload of professors at the London School of Economics. Moreover, Toynbee, besides having no postgraduate supervision, seemed to have 'none of the very heavy examining, essay reading and other paper work to do which burdens many other University professors'. As for the department's Modern Greek teaching this seemed to have been a complete failure: 'Any work done seems to be so elementary that it might be done by a village schoolmaster'. He was sceptical, too, about Toynbee's bibliographical activities.

On the whole, Pember Reeves concluded, the results were clearly so disappointing 'as to warrant plain speaking' on the part of the Subscribers' Committee. The chair's benefactors 'cannot be getting what they hoped or even what they are entitled to'. He wondered whether the lack of activity was an indication of public apathy or whether an improvement might be expected 'if the occupant of the Chair were one who had an enthusiasm for Mediaeval and Modern Greece and real cordiality towards Modern Greeks as a race and Greece as a political entity'.

> At present the Chair is occupied by a gentleman who is regarded by Greeks and those interested in Greece as a persistent and mischievous enemy of the Greek race and cause. His numerous anti-Greek writings and speeches have caused bitter exasperation amongst Greeks and the friends of Greece and from those not unimportant quarters the Koraes Chair is not likely to be supported.

As it seemed to Pember Reeves, Toynbee had gone out of his way to doom the department to failure.[34] At the Subscribers' Committee meeting of 9 March, Eumorfopoulos was empowered to draft a letter embodying the gist of the comments of those present which would then be circulated to the other members of the Committee before being forwarded to King's College. But a furious row was to break out in the Committee as to the tone and timing of this letter.

What appears to have been the first draft of such a letter survives among Gennadius' papers. It was bitterly critical of Toynbee, referring to his 'unmeasured abuse of the Greeks'. Toynbee, it claimed, was known even across the Atlantic 'as the unofficial advocate of the Kemalists'. After accepting their hospitality and winning their favour he 'employed every device known to professional propagandists in decrying, defaming, and damaging the cause of the Greek people .... He suppressed the fact that the acts he so virtuously denounced were really the reprisals of a people goaded to desperation by centuries of unrelenting oppression'. 'While enjoying at home and in travel emoluments derived from a Greek foundation, he accused the Greeks of the crime of burning Smyrna, and in advocating the maintenance of Turkish tyranny called to witness his conscience.' At a meeting of the Foreign Affairs Association 'a distinguished English author and publicist', who was familiar with Near Eastern affairs, had denounced Toynbee as a liar. In the opinion of a number of Englishmen this was not a matter concerning liberty of speech, but one of 'blatant contempt of elementary *bienséance* and of the unwritten law governing the conduct of gentlemen'.[35] On 24 March Eumorfopoulos wrote to Gennadius to say that Pember Reeves had suggested toning down the draft letter to King's College to avoid alienating moderate opinion. The revised letter which he now proposed closely followed Pember Reeves' critique of Toynbee's report to the Subscribers. The new draft declared that the Subscribers had been irresistibly led to 'conclude that a large amount of energetic work in political controversy done by the Professor at the expense of Greek political and ethnical aspirations has caused wide resentment among members of the race by which the Koraes Chair was established and their friends'. In conclusion the Committee declared itself to be 'somewhat embarrassed in endeavouring to understand a mentality which finds it possible to consider the political activities' to which they had adverted as compatible with the tenure of the Koraes Chair.

> The Committee do not dispute the right of holding any political views one may believe in and profess, but the persistent purpose of injuring national causes dear to the heart of all Greeks and of promoting the interests of her enemies – manifested especially after the visit to Constantinople – has caused bitter exasperation among Greeks and their friends.

The next day, 25 March, Gennadius wrote a furious letter of complaint to Eumorfopoulos for having agreed in consultation with Pember Reeves and Marchetti to tone down the letter, thus by-passing the normal functioning of the Subscribers' Committee. The letter had now been 'emasculated in its essentials to such a degree as to suppress all reference to the grave charge broadcast against us Greeks that it was we who set fire to Smyrna'. Gennadius declined to participate in such a retreat, nor was he in favour of any delay in sending the letter pending Toynbee's imminent visit to Athens and Constantinople which might give him the necessary 'respite for the staging of his new impersonation as an ardent Philhellene'. The previous day, 24 March, Gennadius had written to Ionides that he was against any delay which might give Toynbee time 'to show friendship to Greece': 'to seek friendship on such terms from such quarters seems to me impolitic, undignified and suicidal'. Eumorfopoulos replied to Gennadius on 26 March, saying that he did not think there was any need to clear himself of the charge of disloyalty. His meeting with Pember Reeves and Marchetti had not been planned but had arisen out of a chance meeting on the Underground. He did not consider that he was in any way breaking faith with the Committee in revising the letter, after showing it to Pember Reeves and resubmitting it to Gennadius. He now felt that he could no longer remain on the Committee and hence enclosed his letter of resignation.

Gennadius was not to be mollified. As he wrote in reply on 27 March, he had wished all along that the letter be sent in its original form without giving time to Toynbee to 'make public his imminent conversion to phil-hellenism'. Meanwhile, at a 'casual' meeting Eumorfopoulos had 'proceeded to demolish our carefully constructed defence, to make things nice and comfortable for our bitter detractor and assailant. And you expected me to take it all lying down'. His last letter had indicated that he refused to have anything further to do 'with the muddle to which a patriotic duty and worthy purpose had thus been reduced'. It was, therefore, to some other quarter that Eumorfopoulos should address his resignation, which he now returned.[36]

Gennadius, however, subsequently withdrew his threat to have nothing more to do with the Committee on the grounds that he was being kept in the dark about its operations.[37] Eumorfopoulos emerged as the victor in this particular encounter, for not only was a toned down version of the original draft letter sent, but it was held back until mid-May by which time Toynbee had returned from his visit to the Near East. The Committee's considered reply, following the receipt of Toynbee's report, was sent to the Secretary of King's College on 12 May. It began by emphasizing that the Committee's wish to be kept informed of the work of the chair, of which the college authorities were unaware, had been contained in the Committee's official letter of 24 April 1918 to the Principal of King's and had been noted in the minutes of the Senate. The Committee could hardly consider the report a full one for it dealt mainly with the third year's work, that is to say the 1921–22 session. (Toynbee had in fact made it clear in his report of 2 February that he had, to avoid delay, based his report on the annual report for that session which he had prepared for the Principal and which had been circulated to the Professorial Board.)[38] From the report it emerged that during the first year the professor had lectured about once a week, to an unspecified number of students. His professorial work for the second year had finished after he had given ten lectures, thereafter he had spent two terms in the Near East, engaged 'in study and in newspaper work'. In the third year he had given ten academic and ten public lectures, the latter on his experiences in the Near East. The reason why the Principal of King's College had asked him not to give any further public lectures (in his report Toynbee said that the Principal had asked him to 'restrict' the number of public lectures) was not stated, but 'it is known that the tendency and scope of those lectures were not generally considered to harmonise with academic pursuits'. The Committee, therefore, were not surprised to find that the audience for the academic lectures attracted only two students. In the fourth year the professor was to give a mere six academic lectures.

Moreover, it was clear that, besides these lectures, the professor had had none, or almost none, of 'the very heavy examining, essay-reading, and other paper work to do, which burdens generally University Professors', a passage taken almost verbatim from Pember Reeves' letter of 26 February. The seminar on Western travellers in the Near East between 1650 and 1856 was potentially interesting and useful were it to lead to the 'discovery and publication of fresh historic or economic fact' beyond those indicated in six previously published works of this kind, a list of which was appended.[39] The Committee had not been impressed by the work that Toynbee had done for the library. The letter then turned to consider 'the fundamental cause of these manifestly poor results' which resulted from the professor being so manifestly out of sympathy with 'the mentality and the legitimate aspirations' of the people whose history and literature he was teaching. Moreover his other activities were hardly of a friendly nature. The subscribers attributed the very poor attendance at the academic lectures to Toynbee's 'extra-academic publications in magazines and newspapers in favour of Turkey and Bulgaria'. The Committee could not concur with Toynbee's novel view that Modern Greek would be studied in London only 'in a dilettante and desultory way' and that, even in the Levant, Greek came as a 'bad third or fourth' after Russian, Egyptian Arabic or even Turkish. Such extraordinary allegations were incompatible with the acceptance of the chair by its present incumbent. Moreover, the Committee would have regarded it as incredible, were it not recorded in print, that Greek was classed in the Boards of Studies with the Slavonic and Oriental Languages. The inefficiency and weakness displayed had been so marked that the initial interest in the subject had evaporated and eager students had been discouraged.

The Committee's letter then moved to consider what in its considered opinion was a matter of capital importance, namely the attitude taken by the present incumbent of the chair in his political publications and public lectures: 'That attitude has been one of pronounced hostility to Greece, and has amounted to an unequivocal advocacy of the enemies of Greece in the Near East'. The professor had been granted leave to proceed to Greece and the Levant in order to acquaint himself with Modern Greek, which, from the outset had been considered a necessary qualification for the post. (Toynbee, of course, already had a good knowledge of Modern Greek deriving from his sojourn in Greece in 1911–12.) To what extent he had acquired the necessary knowledge of the language was not clear 'but it is a matter of public notoriety that, especially since his return from Constantinople, he has figured as one of the bitterest critics of the Greeks, and to such an extent as to make it difficult to discriminate between him, as an Englishman, and the professional advocates of Turkey'. 'The mis-statements and misrepresentations to which he has given currency must affect even his status as an historian. It would be an unpleasant task to review the rough and unedifying field of his propagandist activities' but the Committee thought that one of the many instances should be mentioned. This was his insinuation that it was the Greeks who had set fire to Smyrna, 'the native town of Koraes himself', following the rout of the Greek armies in September 1922.[40] This charge had been made in the face of overwhelming evidence to the contrary.

One would have expected from him, if only on the score of historic importance, some comment on the harrowing events unprecedented in history which are so tragically connected with the displacement of a million and a half of souls in circumstances of unexampled barbarity.

The Committee found itself somewhat embarrassed in trying to understand the mentality which found it possible to regard such propagandistic activities as compatible with the tenure of the Koraes Chair. While the Committee did not dispute the right to hold political views of any kind, 'the persistent purpose of injuring Greece and her cause and of promoting the interest of her enemies ... has caused bitter exasperation' not only among Greeks 'but in those English circles which maintain as an honourable heirloom the noble tradition of phil-Hellenism'. There were certain moral obligations which were especially incumbent upon a gentleman and a scholar and in the present case a choice should have been made between championing the cause of the Turk and Bulgar and the holding of the Koraes Chair. The Committee very much doubted whether professors of French, Spanish and Slavonic would have acted in similar circumstances without resigning. The Committee wished to remind the university authorities of the purposes for which the Koraes endowment had been established and which should not be used 'for the maintenance of a prolific source of injury to Greece'. In conclusion the Committee respectfully asked the university authorities whether 'they considered that the continuance of Professor Toynbee in the Koraes Chair is compatible with the object of its foundation and the purposes for the advancement of which this Fund was created'.[41] Out of fairness to Toynbee, the Committee had delayed sending the letter to the college authorities until his return from his recent visit to the Near East.

As soon as a copy of the Committee's letter had been passed on to him, Toynbee wrote to Gilbert Murray for advice. Murray on 16 May counselled Toynbee that the letter had clearly been 'meant to make you resign: therefore you ought to think twice before doing so'. 'Undoubtedly one's first reaction is to say "take your damned chair and give it to a Greek propagandist" '. Toynbee seems to have intimated to Murray that he was thinking of resigning and taking up a journalistic career, for Murray wrote that in his view it would be a mistake 'to allow yourself to be drawn into even high-class journalism as a permanent thing'. On the following day, 17 May, Murray wrote to Barker that Eumorfopoulos' letter of the 12th had been deliberately insulting. On the other hand he had felt even before this letter some doubts as to whether Toynbee should remain in the chair 'considering that though his intellectual judgement is, I think, remarkably impartial, his emotional sympathies are with the Turks rather than with the Greeks'. While it was true that the chair had been founded for the purposes of academic study rather than propaganda, it was none the less 'quite natural that the donors should feel hurt and even ill-treated, if the Professor whom they are supporting is markedly out of sympathy with their point of view'. He accepted that Barker's position was more difficult. Murray's advice was that he should reject the Committee's claim for detailed supervision of the chair and if the donors were under the impression that they should have this control then the endowment should be returned. Such a move would put both the college and Toynbee in a more dignified position. During the next few days Toynbee seems to have taken the decision to resign for on 30 May his mother wrote to him that the news that he was resigning was a positive relief: 'For a long time now I have felt very strongly that the post was an impossible one for anyone, and most of all so for you with your strong Turkish sympathies'. The subscribers could not consider him an impartial observer rather than a partisan. '... I won't promise not to think that you may be a little obsessed with your Turks.' A fortnight later she wrote to suggest to Toynbee that he might try to retain the chair, provided that it meant not dishonesty but rather being 'non-provocative, not-aggressive, and perhaps a little less of the Turk champion'. The news that Toynbee had decided to resign quickly reached the ears of the Subscribers' Committee and on 3 June Eumorfopoulos wrote to Gennadius that he had heard confidentially from Professor Gardner[42] and from Mavrogordato that Toynbee had on several occasions tried to resign but that Barker had rejected the offer and 'even induced him to abstain from making public the fact that he wished to resign'. The reason for this was that Barker did not want the question of conscience to be raised before the Senate so that 'the whole odium of the situation has fallen on Toynbee'. This, Eumorfopoulos wrote, did 'in a way give Toynbee the credit of realising the position' even if it did not say much for his firmness of purpose.[43]

Meanwhile Principal Barker, who on 14 May had courteously acknowledged the receipt of Eumorfopoulos' letter of the 12th, wrote again on 30 May to Eumorfopoulos that he had made a report to the Delegacy of King's College on the whole matter and that, as this report had involved a reference to the Senate, the matter would have to be placed before it. Until the Senate had considered the matter he could not reply to the substance of Eumorfopoulos' letter.[44] In his report to the Delegacy Barker drew attention to the Subscribers' Committee's letters of 26 January and 12 May and suggested that the necessary conditions for free academic work were absent when an external committee, of whose existence he had until recently been unaware, claimed the right to criticize both the work and opinions of a professor. In his view a professor was responsible only to the university. He had therefore asked the advice of the Delegacy. The Delegacy recommended that the Senate should either return the endowment on the ground that, if an external committee were to claim the right of controlling the work and opinions of the professor, then the endowment was incompatible with the traditions and spirit of a university. Failing this, it recommended that the Senate should inform the Subscribers' Commitee that it could not recognize any authority except itself as empowered to control the conduct of a professor of the university. The Delegacy noted that Barker had received an assurance from Toynbee that if the endowment were returned he would simultaneously tender his resignation.[45]

The Delegacy's recommendation was then forwarded for consideration by the Professoriate Committee of the Senate, to whose meeting of 25 June Toynbee was invited to attend,[46] although apparently not for the whole proceedings. For on the following day Barker wrote to Toynbee that the Professoriate Committee had agreed with the policy of the Delegacy, which was in effect the policy that 'Murray and you and I had agreed upon'. He assumed that the Academic Council and the Finance Committee of the Senate would accept the Professoriate Committee's report and that the Senate would give its final approval. Once this process had been completed he took it that a letter would be sent to the Subscribers' Committee stating that in the university's view the Koraes Professor must be free to form his own opinions and to state his own views 'alike in matters of history and in matters of politics, the two (as you said) being closely and inextricably mixed'. If the Subscribers' Committee accepted this contention, then Toynbee would stay on as professor. If it refused, then the university would return the endowment to the Committee at the end of the 1923–24 session, when Toynbee's initial five-year appointment expired.[47] If Toynbee were to find himself in a position to stay on then he would be appointed until retirement on the expiry of his initial five-year term.[48]

The Senate duly considered the report of the Professoriate Committee, as adopted by the Academic Council, on 18 July. The Professoriate Committee had considered the Subscribers' Committee's letter of 12 May to King's College, together with the report drawn up by Barker for the Delegacy. It reported that although the Senate had not, in terms, agreed to submit a triennial report to the subscribers, neither it nor the authorities at King's had taken exception to the request. The response of the Subscribers' Committee had, however, offered criticisms that were only indirectly connected with the work of the chair. These concerned 'opinions the Professor had expressed, principally in articles in the Press, on recent happenings in the Near East, and on certain experiences with which he met while travelling in the East'. It was Toynbee's communications to the *Manchester Guardian*, 'communications which he has told us that he felt himself compelled to make', which had apparently first given rise to criticism on the part of sympathizers with the Greek cause. The Committee did not feel called upon to pronounce on Toynbee's opinions 'except to say that they believe them to be conscientiously entertained by him, and that in the circumstances it was natural that he should desire to find expression for them'. Indeed on two or three occasions these opinions had been asked for by the press and the Committee appreciated Toynbee's contention that silence on his part would have given rise to unfavourable comment. Toynbee felt this so strongly that he would rather resign his chair than hold it in conditions which imposed a veto on his freedom of speech. The Committee believed that a chair whose principal object was to promote the study of Modern Greek history and language must inevitably to some extent impinge upon modern political questions. Aside from this the Committee had been assured that 'in questions of philology no less than history there are in Greece differences of opinion which are not treated as differences in points of scholarship, but are matters of violent political feeling'. It was thus not easy for the holder of such a chair to avoid charges of partisanship.

In the light of the Professoriate Committee's report, the Senate called on the Principal Officer, Sir Cooper Perry, to send the Senate's considered reply to the Subscribers' Committee.[49] In this letter of 19 July, addressed to Eumorfopoulos, Cooper Perry began by stating that the Senate had now had

the opportunity to consider the Subscribers' Committee's letter of 12 May,
together with the report of the Professoriate Committee which had interviewed the Principal of King's College and Professor Toynbee. The Senate
had desired Cooper Perry at once to express his regret that 'through an
unfortunate oversight' the Subscribers' Committee had not been furnished
earlier with the Scheme of Work and Report for which they had asked when
offering the endowment in 1918. The Principal of King's College would be
replying in detail to the Committee's criticisms of Toynbee as a professor.
The Senate had been assured, however, that Toynbee had 'given complete
satisfaction to the authorities of the College to which the Koraes Chair is
attached, and that he has discharged his duties in a manner creditable to the
University and to himself'. As to Toynbee's views on political matters he had
been desired to observe 'that it is contrary to the spirit and tradition of the
University to interfere with the political opinions held by any of its Professors or Teachers'.

> The Senate feel that it would be incompatible with the freedom which a
> University Teacher should enjoy if he were liable to be hampered in
> the free expression of his political opinions, even though criticism
> came from the body to whom the University is under an obligation of
> regard and gratitude for providing much of the endowment of the
> Chair.

Toynbee had expressed his willingness to place his resignation at the
disposal of the Senate. Should a vacancy occur then it would be open to the
Subscribers' Committee, in accordance with the stipulations in its letter of 24
April 1918, to state whether it wished to alter the conditions attaching to the
next professorship or whether it wished to withdraw the fund from the
control of the university. The Senate, of course, was at liberty to give up the
chair if any proposed changes were to prove unacceptable.

> The Senate would view with regret the discontinuance of the Chair
> founded by the generosity of the Greek community, but they feel that
> in the circumstances the Subscribers' Committee may wish to be given
> the opportunity to avail themselves of their right to withdraw the fund
> from the control of the University on a vacancy occurring in the
> Professorship.

In any case the professor must always be responsible to the Senate as the
supreme authority of the university.

> ... So great is the importance which the Senate attach to the necessity
> of a University Professor being free to carry on his work as he thinks
> best, and to express his opinions in political and other matters, that
> they could not agree to the continuance of the Koraes Chair under
> conditions inconsistent with such freedom.[50]

On the same day, 19 July, Barker wrote to Eumorfopoulos with a detailed
reply to the Committee's criticisms of Toynbee's work as Koraes Professor.
He began by emphasizing that he, the Secretary of the College (both of
whom had taken up their appointments after 1918) and Toynbee had all

been unaware of the stipulations attaching to the chair. Nor had they been aware of the continued existence of the Subscribers' Committee. Toynbee had done his utmost, with energy and eagerness, to spread knowledge of his subject. The difficulty he had experienced in attracting students was not his alone but had been experienced by the Professors of Russian (Sir Bernard Pares) and Central European History (R.W. Seton-Watson). No-one had striven harder than Toynbee to promote his subject. Toynbee's report of 2 February had not been a full report, but had, in the interests of avoiding delay, been largely based on his annual report for 1921–22. When Barker had received the report the previous October (1922) he had been so impressed by it that he had done an unusual thing in having it typed and circulated to every member of the Professorial Board at the College as it contained a fine record of endeavour and demonstrated the extent to which teachers of the less mainstream subjects, despite the handicaps under which they laboured, were doing 'loyal service and bringing credit to the College and University'.

Barker then went on to explain that, contrary to the Committee's letter of 12 May, there had never been any prohibition on Toynbee's giving public lectures. Not only had there been no such ban but it would not have been within his power to impose one. What had happened was simple. The Public Lectures Committee of the Professorial Board had felt that there were too many public lectures and that some retrenchment was called for. Toynbee had acted on the suggestion because attendance at his public lectures had not been large. As for the poor attendance by undergraduates at Toynbee's lectures, it was a regrettable fact that London students, unlike their Oxford counterparts, were unwilling to attend lectures that were not obviously of practical utility in their final examinations. The Committee's comments on Toynbee's seminar on 'Western Travellers in the Near East between 1650 and 1856' were also wide of the mark. Toynbee has assured him that the areas covered in the list of works appended to the Subscribers' Committee letter neither clashed with nor anticipated the work he was attempting to do. Barker made the point that in seeking to encourage the study of Central and Eastern Europe and also of the Middle East, the college had attempted to work on a regional basis. Toynbee had worked along these lines and had done his best to cover the whole regional area 'within which Greek civilization has worked and spread'.

> In such academic matters the Professors concerned are naturally and necessarily autonomous, and the development of their studies depends on such autonomy. The authorities of the College have done nothing, because they have no right to do anything, to control or to check such development.

Moreover, the assignment of the Koraes Professor to membership of the Boards of Studies in Slavonic and Oriental Languages exactly followed the analogy of the University of Paris.

He concluded by remarking that 'the historical aspect and the broad historical scope of Professor Toynbee's work are exactly in accordance with the communications which he had with my predecessor, Dr

Burrows, which I have seen and studied'. He had been assured by
Toynbee that he had always attempted to make his historical work
specifically Byzantine or Modern Greek and that he had been drawn
into broader themes only at the urgent request of colleagues.

> My last and most earnest word is this: I have been a teacher myself for
> nearly 25 years; I have known Professor Toynbee for the greater part
> of that period; I have always admired his scholarship; I am proud that
> he should be my colleague; and, judged by the highest standard of
> scholarship which I can set, he has not in my view been wanting in any
> particular or on any point in his academic work, to which I have
> confined all the observations I have made.

The letter was typewritten and the last phrase 'in his academic work, to
which I have confined all the observations I have made', was written in
Barker's own hand.[51]

The Subscribers' Committee was in no hurry to respond to the letters from
Cooper Perry and Barker, not least because communication with the
members of the Committee was difficult during the summer months. Toynbee was thus left in suspense, not knowing whether the Committee would
decide to accept the university's offer to return the endowment, in which
case he would be without a job. In October he wrote to the Academic
Registrar of the university to see whether there had been any response, but
Deller replied that, although he could well understand Toynbee's anxiety,
he did not think that there was any use in trying to worry the Committee. At
much the same time Toynbee wrote to Mavrogordato to ask whether he had
news of any developments.[52]

During the summer, however, Eumorfopoulos was taking soundings from
the members of the Committee, and others, as how next to proceed. One of
the outsiders who weighed in with advice, at Eumorfopoulos' request, was
Harold Spender, a member of the Executive Commitee of the Anglo-
Hellenic League.[53] He advocated taking a strong line with the university,
and that the subscribers should exercise their option to withdraw the
endowment. It was, he believed, quite clear that the university had no
sympathy with the objects of the chair and that Barker could not be trusted
to control Toynbee. Any university that refused to exercise any control over
the political activities of its members reduced 'the whole of its academic
activities to a possible farce'. In such circumstances it would be possible for a
professor of English to become 'a notorious and emblazoned enemy of this
country, engaged in open propaganda'. He thought it pointless to continue
the argument with Barker for his complaint against Toynbee had never been
based on shortcomings in lectures or research. It was impossible to acquire
sufficient knowledge on this score to press the attack and in any case the
standards accepted by King's College could never be determined. That was
clearly a domestic matter for the college to decide.

> Do not shift your ground [he wrote] or be frightened from the real
> heart of your criticism. The case of Professor Toynbee is gross. His

'offence is rank, and cries to Heaven'. It is that having accepted a Greek chair, founded by Greeks with a Greek endowment, he has used most of his energies, and resources, and all his spare time, to conduct a virulent and sustained attack on the Greek nation in their hour of utmost peril. He has also gone to Angora and engaged in close and friendly colloquies with the enemies of Greece. If you cannot resent that, and cannot show your resentment by the most drastic and vigorous action, you will be unworthy of your traditions.[54]

The Committee should agree to Toynbee's resignation, suspend the chair and give the endowment to a university more fit to control it.

By no means all of those whom Eumorfopoulos consulted were so convinced that the Committee should take a hard line. On 18 August Eumorfopoulos wrote to Gennadius (unusually in Greek and from Newquay) that although Mitaranga and Petrocochino were in agreement with the Committee's action he had heard from Alexander Pallis in Athens that he was inclined to the view that it would have been better not to take any steps against Toynbee. 'It looks now as if we had objected to him as a Professor because politically he disapproved of us. It looks, in other words, like spite.' Andreades, on the other hand, had written that whereas he had previously been of the view that it was better to leave Toynbee alone he had since changed his mind. He recommended writing to the university to the effect that Toynbee's resignation was the correct solution but at the same time he stressed that the Committee should not claim a right of control over the teaching of the chair and that the subscribers had no right to expect the professor to be a Philhellene.[55] Early in October Eumorfopoulos, in the light of the advice he had received, circulated a draft reply to the Senate, to be considered at a meeting of the Subscribers' Committee called for 24 October. Among those circulated was Harold Spender who predictably approved of its tough line although he thought the reply should have been sent while the matter was 'hot on the anvil, instead of waiting until it was cold'. 'You *Professors* are always *late*' [Eumorfopoulos taught physics, it will be remembered, at University College], he wrote '... but they are Professors also: and they will not expect you to be otherwise than late: and would indeed have been very upset if you had been in a hurry, or even in time.' Apart from this, however, he was in entire agreement with the letter and hoped that they would see the last of Toynbee 'whose recent attempts to come in at the last moment after the debacle as the true friend of Greece only excite my contempt'.[56] What these attempts were is not altogether clear. Certainly, however, Toynbee had written, 'as a strong opponent of Greek conduct and aims in Anatolia', on 12 September to the *The Times*, commending Greece's restrained behaviour over the Corfu incident, which was in the interests not only of Greece but of international order. This crisis arose from Mussolini's bombardment and occupation of Corfu, following the shooting of an Italian member of the Greek/Albanian frontier commission.[57] On the reverse of his draft of this letter, preserved among his papers, Toynbee had written that he was about to be consulted by a representative of Cyprus as to how best the British public might be persuaded that Cyprus ought to be united to Greece. The saving grace of the Near East, he wrote, was that there was always some comic relief.

Eumorfopoulos in a letter of 20 October to Gennadius also reported that Mitaranga had written to him on 12 October that he would prefer that the entire endowment be returned and the income used, under the direction of the Committee, to underwrite 'Greek propaganda of a useful and international character'. In a subsequent letter of 15 October to Eumorfopoulos, Mitaranga said that he had come across a critical review of the *Western Question* in the *Journal of Hellenic Studies*.[58] Given that the Society for the Promotion of Hellenic Studies was carrying on 'a most praiseworthy and at the same time ungrateful work', with extremely meagre means, and that its board was composed of 'men of mark' in their line and was well equipped for lectures, it had occurred to him that the Committee *might* come to an understanding with the Society and, 'on certain terms, advantageous to both parties but fulfilling the Committee's requirements', grant part of the fund's income to the Society.[59] Two days later, on 22 October, Eumorfopoulos forwarded to Gennadius Petrocochino's comments on the draft letter. He considered the reply to be excellent and the decision to accept Toynbee's resignation to be quite right. His only reservation was that he thought the passage 'accusations which have been proved to have been without foundation', following a reference to Toynbee's violent and bitter accusations against the Greeks, to be rather sweeping 'as, unfortunately, our countrymen did behave badly on many occasions in Asia Minor'. Petrocochino also did not think the letter laid sufficient stress on what he thought to be very essential, namely 'the theories of Toynbee about Greek mentality and literary and artistic production, as compared with Turkish – which render the existence of the Chair absolutely useless'.[60]

The draft letter was duly considered at a meeting of the Subscribers' Committee, held on 24 October and attended by Gennadius, Marchetti and Eumorfopoulos. One of the few amendments agreed was to delete the passage which Petrocochino had thought injudicious, the reference to accusations against the Greeks 'which have been proved to have been without foundation'. The amended version was duly sent to Cooper Perry by Eumorfopoulos the following day, 25 October. He apologized for the delay, which had been occasioned by the holiday period and the absence of many members of the Committee from town. The delay had not, however, 'in any sense modified the views which the Committee expressed in their previous communication, nor has it altered the position of the matter before us'. The Committee entirely took the point that the Senate could not interfere with the political opinions of teachers at the university. What they took exception to was that

> Professor Toynbee, having accepted a Greek chair, founded by Greeks, with a Greek endowment, and graced by the illustrious name of Koraes, has used most of his energies, resources, and spare time to conduct a virulent and sustained attack on the Greek nation in its hour of utmost peril. He has also gone to Angora and engaged in close and friendly understanding with our enemies, to the propagation of whose interests he has devoted his enthusiastic endeavours.

The Committee's view was shared by a large and influential body of Englishmen 'whose traditions and principles would never lead them to interfere with political opinions honestly and righteously held, but who would consider it impossible for a Professor of English, occupying a Chair endowed with English funds, to become a notorious and emblazoned enemy of England, engaged in open propaganda against her', phraseology originally employed by Spender. Toynbee had neither withdrawn, nor apologized for, his violent and bitter accusations against the Greeks. He claimed authority on Near Eastern matters on account of his visits to, and acceptance of the hospitality of, Mustafa Kemal and 'his imputations, coming from the Koraes Professor, are quoted as evidence against Greece'. The Committee did not propose to respond to Principal Barker's letter of 19 July which they saw as 'but a generous endeavour to shield a fellow-professor'. It inferred from Cooper Perry's letter of the same date that Professor Toynbee 'so far realises the incompatibility of his tenure of the Koraes Chair with his political activities as to tender his resignation'. While appreciating the embarrassment that Professor Toynbee's activities must have caused the Senate, the Committee entertained the confident hope that they would be informed that his resignation had been accepted.[61]

The Committee's uncompromising reply left no room for manoeuvre. Toynbee now had no option but to go ahead with his resignation. On 6 November he wrote to Barker to confirm his offer to resign from the Koraes Chair which had been placed in the hands of the Professoriate Committee at its meeting of 25 June, to which he had been invited to attend. At the same time he reserved the right to make a public statement explaining his reasons for so resigning. He enclosed a draft of the kind of statement he had in mind in case the university wished to see it. He had no fear of being thought a knave save by partisans for he had, after all, lost his position as a result of exposing facts and expressing opinions to which he had felt obliged to testify. Rather he was afraid of being thought to have accepted the chair blindly, whereas if he had been aware of the stipulations attaching to it he would not have applied.[62] At this juncture Toynbee was in touch with Graham Wallas, Professor of Political Science at the London School of Economics, who was to prove one of his staunchest supporters on the Senate. After reading the original correspondence between Toynbee and the University, Wallas wrote on 15 November to Copper Perry to say that he felt unhappy about the way in which the university had treated him 'especially since he is a married man with a young family and no immediate prospect of more work'. It was clear to him that Toynbee's appointment had been made without any reference to the rights of the Greek Committee. Burrows' letter of 25 April 1919 could have had no other meaning to him than that 'the committee was *functus officio* and had nothing further to do with the appointment'. He had only accepted the chair on the distinct terms that he was to be an historian 'and was neither Philhellene nor AntiHellene at the time of his appointment'. Toynbee, in Wallas' view, was 'very much of an idealist and makes light of his own grievances'.

A few days later, on 18 November, Toynbee wrote to Wallas to thank him for his 'extraordinarily kind interest in the matter' and to discuss possible outcomes to the dispute. Given that it was out of the question that the donors would reconcile themselves both to resigning control of the chair and to his remaining as Koraes Professor, he believed that the least objectionable course would be for the endowment to be returned, either on the university's initiative or else through his creating a vacancy by resignation, in which case the donors would be empowered to withdraw the endowment. Contrary to what was usually the case he felt the two middle courses to be distinctly the least desirable. The first of these was that the university and he

> should, so to speak combine to defy the Greeks on behalf of academic freedom .... The weak point of this is that the donors, after all, gave their money on another understanding, which, however unfortunate, was the fact. As it is, they have not enjoyed their control; and if what Eumorfopoulos told Barker is the case and they really wanted a professor of the literature, my original appointment, in the circumstances, was hardly justifiable. This being so, I feel that this line would put both the University and me in too invidious a position.

The second course would be for the university to come to terms with the donors, with the donors agreeing to waive their control provided that he had been eliminated as professor. 'Strictly it is outside my province to discuss this, and I have given my resignation without any reserve except the liberty to make a public statement'. But such a course would be a bargain at Toynbee's expense, with the university using the incidental fact that he was *persona ingratissima* to the donors to obtain release from awkward terms, which he himself had not been given the chance to steer clear of. As to the future, he was well aware that the university would be unable to pay a professor's salary to enable him to continue his work but he wondered whether it might be possible to arrange a joint lectureship at King's and the School of Oriental Studies so that he could 'keep at least a minimum continuity with the study and teaching of Near Eastern history'.[63]

Meanwhile, Barker was coming under very strong pressure from a group within the college, led by R.W. Seton-Watson, the Masaryk Professor of Central European History, to do whatever he could to salvage the chair, and not to return the endowment if Toynbee were eventually forced to resign as the Principal had originally determined with Toynbee and Murray. The motives of Seton-Watson and those of like mind appear to have been threefold. They thought that Toynbee had clearly overstepped the mark in his tenure of the chair and felt very strongly that a chair so closely associated with the late Principal Burrows should, if at all possible, be preserved in his memory. They feared, moreover, that the quarrel with the donors of the Koraes endowment might threaten the whole edifice of subsidy on which the School of Slavonic Studies was based. In 1923, for instance, the total income of the School amounted to between £4,000 and £5,000, of which some £1,200 came from foreign governments. The Czech government provided £300 for the maintenance of the lectureship in Czech and Slovak and a further £400 as half of the endowment of the Masaryk Chair of Central European History[64] and had undertaken to pay the full cost of the endowment, £800 for the 1924–25 session.

A further annual grant of £250 was paid by the government of the Kingdom of the Serbs, Croats and Slovenes for a lectureship in Serbo-Croat, with another £250 being paid by the Polish authorities for the maintenance during the current year of a lectureship in Polish, with the possibility of this subsidy being made permanent.[65] Not the least of the odd aspects of the whole astonishing story is that, just as the whole Toynbee affair was coming to a head, King's College should have been considering the establishment of a lectureship in the history of Romania and the Near East with a subvention from the Romanian government of £350 per annum for three years in the first instance. At a meeting of the Professorial Board of King's College of 5 December 1923, a letter making the offer from Nicolae Titulescu, the Romanian minister in London, was discussed and a committee, which included Barker and Seton-Watson, 'with power if they think fit to make a recommendation to the Delegacy for a definite appointment' was established. Negotiations on the matter took place between Barker and Titulescu, who, in June 1924, wrote to confirm that the Romanian government would, for the next three years, make available £350 per annum for a lectureship in the history of Romania and the Near East, to be held by Wickham Steed, the foreign editor of *The Times*, and £200 per annum for a part-time lectureship, to be held by Marcu Beza, a Vlach from Kleisoura, in Romanian language and literature.[66]

Seton-Watson wrote to Principal Barker at some time in the first half of November, when Toynbee's decision to resign had become final, protesting, in Barker's words, 'with vigour against any dropping of the endowment or cessation of the Chair' and arguing that the conditions, such as they were, stipulated by the Subscribers' Committee were not unreasonable.[67] In this letter, an undated draft of which survives, Seton-Watson said that Toynbee had been to see him about the furore and had asked him to talk over the points he had raised with George Glasgow as representing Burrows' friends. Glasgow, a part-time teacher and freelance journalist, had acted as a subeditor for *The New Europe*, and was engaged at this time in writing a life of Burrows, which was published in 1924 under the title *Ronald Burrows: A Memoir*.[68] Glasgow was clearly devoted to Burrows' memory and regarded the Koraes Chair as his main memorial. Toynbee had shown Seton-Watson Burrows' letter of 25 April 1919 in answer to Toynbee's query soon after his election about possible dissatisfaction on the part of the donors with his appointment. (A copy of this letter, in Toynbee's own hand, is preserved in the Seton-Watson papers.) Toynbee had concluded from this letter, and in particular from the handwritten addition of the phrase 'at this stage', that Burrows had been deliberately concealing from him certain essential facts regarding the Chair, which, had he been aware of them, would have led to his withdrawing his candidature. 'This view strikes me as a real mare's nest, but with Toynbee it appears to be an *idée fixe*.' Seton-Watson, however, had kept all the relevant documents and was able to give Toynbee chapter and verse for his interpretation. As early as 26 April 1918 Burrows had notified those concerned with the establishment of the chair that the subscribers had renounced their hitherto rather stringent conditions and were now prepared to hand over the endowment on one condition only, namely that, on the

chair becoming vacant, the Subscribers' Committee should be entitled to
reconsider the conditions attaching to it and possibly its continued existence.
Burrows had stated that he personally would have preferred to dispense with
this condition but he had regarded this concession as the minimum necessary
to secure the endowment. In any case, he had argued, the fact that the
agreement of a two-thirds majority of the Subscribers' Committee was
necessary before any change could be made in the conditions implied that
the endowment could, in practice, be regarded as permanent. As for the
stipulation regarding a triennial report Seton-Watson argued that this had
been a mere 'wish' on the part of the subscribers, not a condition.

It therefore seemed clear to Seton-Watson that no 'conditions' or 'control'
existed, other than those contained in the regulations printed by the
university in May 1918. 'The suggestion that Burrows was trying to keep
back something essential from Toynbee's knowledge, is not only entirely
contrary to his whole character, but such an action would have been at
lowest preposterously silly, as he could not have calculated on essential facts
remaining unknown to the holder of the Chair for any length of time and
then discovery would obviously lead to trouble.' What Burrows might have
had in mind by using the phrase 'at this stage' was that the Subscribers'
Committee would only have any say when a vacancy had arisen. As for the
Committee's wish for periodical reports this appeared to Seton-Watson to
be entirely natural and proper, for it was 'hardly to be expected that a body
of donors should disinterest themselves entirely in the working of their
foundation'. He took it that it was the accident of Burrows' death and of no-
one informing Barker as his successor that this wish was not acted upon. To
Seton-Watson it was quite obvious, 'although it would be unkind to throw
this in Toynbee's face' and he had therefore not mentioned it in conversation, that Burrows, 'if he had even remotely foreseen such action on the part
of the Professor as Toynbee's during 1920–23, would never have accepted
Toynbee as a candidate at all'.

The main point on which Seton-Watson was anxious to insist was that the
question as to whether Burrows had withheld essential information had no
connection whatever with the issue as to whether the chair should continue
to exist after Toynbee's resignation.

> This question, which, to my amazement and horror, I gather is present
> in Toynbee's mind, is one which all Burrows' friends would feel bound
> to take up – I in particular, as a member of the original Board of
> Advisors and one with whom Burrows discussed every stage of the
> Chair's genesis.

Now that Toynbee had resigned, the sole problem faced by the university
was that of securing a successor who enjoyed sufficient prestige to make
good Toynbee's 'deplorable blunder'.

> The very idea that the University or College could repudiate its
> obligations towards Greece, simply because the candidate it appointed
> conducted an active political campaign against Greece and so found
> himself in an untenable position is one which I do not like to con-

template: and I hope that perhaps after all it only exists in Toynbee's imagination. I am exceedingly sorry for Toynbee but I do not see that he has a leg to stand upon.[69]

On 16 November Barker replied to Seton-Watson that he was doing his best to set matters straight in the matter of the Koraes Chair. He feared that he disagreed ('you must forgive me for doing so'), however, on one point. He did consider that the Subscribers' Committee's conditions were impossible in a university and could not really be continued. Provided they were withdrawn or so modified as to be innocuous he would do his best to ensure the continuance of the chair. 'If the Greek Committee will not budge I honestly fear that my conscience will impel me to be a Trojan and to fight the Greeks.' He was in any case to see Glasgow soon and hoped that matters would not reach that stage.[70] In his letter of (?) 24 November to Toynbee, Barker wrote that, in the opinion of the lawyers, the university was free to return the money to the Greeks but that he was coming under pressure from Seton-Watson and Glasgow. He was, he said, torn between two conflicting emotions – 'the desire to vindicate you and the principles for which you have stood (even though, as I must frankly confess, I think you have carried it a long way), and the desire to maintain a chair, *provided it is a free chair*, which deals with Byzantine and Modern Greek History and Literature'. The second wish was reinforced by his feeling of piety towards his predecessor, Burrows, 'who put his heart into this particular thing, even if (as I still think, even after Seton-Watson's letter) he went wrong in the way in which he handled it'. On 27 November Toynbee thanked Barker for this letter and for what he had told him on the previous day of the views of the Delegacy. He had no objection, if the endowment were returned and the Delegacy wished to provide further funds on its own account, to the Delegacy's wish that this be earmarked for literature and language and not history. But in this case the matter should be explained, otherwise such a move would reflect on Toynbee by implying that he had failed in his academic duty. Toynbee had always made it clear that he intended to specialize in history, to which Burrows had agreed. Moreover, Burrows' first choice had always been Miller who was definitely a historian.[71]

On 25 November Eumorfopoulos wrote to Gennadius to report on his recent contacts with Barker. He had told Barker that the subscribers, after their experience with Toynbee, were unwilling to give up their right of criticism. When he had complained to Barker that the College had made no apparent effort to curtail Toynbee's activities Barker had told him ('confidentially, of course') that this was not correct. Some months before the receipt of the Committee's letter of complaint and remonstrance of 26 January 1923, a few of Toynbee's colleagues had spoken earnestly to him, asking him to desist or at least publish under a pseudonym, but he would not listen. Barker feared that the university would return the endowment although he was anxious that they should not do so lest this be taken as a reflection on Burrows' memory. On the next day, 26 November, however, Eumorfopoulos wrote to Gennadius to say that Glasgow had told him that morning that he thought Barker was quite ready to undo part of Burrows' work and get rid of the Koraes Chair. Eumorfopoulos suspected some intrigue, although that was perhaps too strong a word.[72] Arising from these contacts between Eumorfopoulos and Barker, it was agreed to organize an informal meeting of the Principal with the Subscribers' Committee for 4 December and, on 28 November, Gennadius suggested to Eumorfopoulos that it would be advisable if those attending gathered half an hour earlier to concert a common line for the meeting with Barker. At this hour-long meeting, however, attended by four members of the Committee, among them Gennadius, there was no indication that the Committee was prepared to move from its hard line and drop what Barker termed 'the obnoxious conditions' attached to the Chair. For on 9 December he wrote to Seton-Watson to explain that there had been no sign of movement on the Committee's part. From the way things were going he believed that the Senate would decide to accept Toynbee's resignation, at the same time returning the endowment. He, personally, had always believed that the university would be driven to return the endowment, although he had tried hard for the sake of Burrows' memory to reach an accommodation. He could not see what further action he could take. He could not oppose in the Senate action resolved upon by a Senate Committee after the most prolonged consideration that he had ever seen given to an issue.[73]

The inflexibility of the Committee's stance, and its unwillingness to compromise, is reflected in Gennadius' long account of a meeting he had in mid-December with Burrows' widow, Una, in the presence of his wife. Mrs Burrows, Gennadius wrote, was in full sympathy and agreement with the subscribers' views. None the less, because of the danger threatening the chair, which she regarded as a monument to her husband's memory, she thought the Committee should be prepared to make certain concessions along the lines proposed by Barker and Glasgow. Gennadius had felt that he could only repeat the reply he had given at the Committee's meeting with Barker, namely that the future of the chair could not be considered in isolation before there had been a solution to the matter of Toynbee. 'We could not stultify ourselves, and prove unfaithful to the trust placed in our keeping, by shifting our ground, or by bargaining away its very essence.' Were the academic authorities to content themselves merely with the voluntary retirement of Toynbee on the expiry of his five-year term that would be tantamount to a declaration that they found nothing reprehensible in the proceedings against which the Committee had protested. Toynbee would then be allowed to make his exit 'with colours flying'. Moreover, a number of English gentlemen and scholars had warned the Committee that, if it did not vigorously insist on his being called to account, then it would in effect be confirming his strictures against the Greek nation. Toynbee claimed liberty of speech and freedom of opinion, but even the British Parliament, the very sanctuary of free speech, had hedged that freedom with the most stringent safeguards and limitations: 'for unchequed [sic], vitious [sic] and malevolent attack is not liberty but abuse of speech'. 'Moreover this man, Toynbee, is quoted by all the enemies and detractors of Greece as an authority, by the very fact that he holds the Koraes chair and enjoys a salary derived from a Greek foundation.' 'We will not bargain away our just cause', he thundered. The future arrangements pertaining to the chair would be duly considered at the proper time and in normal circumstances. As a first priority, the matter of the 'savage, perfidious and dishonourable propaganda carried on against the Greek people by a man who first became known on his appointment to a Greek chair and on his receiving a Greek salary, must first be settled on its own merits'. He placed the onus of a 'just and satisfactory' decision fairly and squarely on the academic authorities. Gennadius' wife had agreed with every word he had said, and Mrs Burrows herself, he maintained, had been constrained to admit the justice and force of his remarks.[74]

Meanwhile the matter had been placed on the agenda of the meeting of the Senate to be held on 19 December. On 9 December Barker wrote to Toynbee to say that he intended to speak for him at this meeting, making it clear that Toynbee had been unaware of the existence of the Subscribers' Committee and of its conception of the duties of the chair as expressed in the Senate Minute of May 1918, of its wish for sessional programmes and a triennial report, together with the right to make 'criticisms and suggestions thereon', and of its power to modify these conditions on a vacancy. He also intended to make clear that Toynbee had offered to resign in both 1921 and 1922 and that he had been ready to welcome any suggestion from Barker on that point. The Senate would be informed and he would be left free to decide whether he wished to publish such information '*urbi et orbi*'.[75]

At the 19 December meeting of the Senate the report of the Professoriate Committee was considered. This gave the text of Eumorfopoulos' letter of 25 October, together with the counsel's opinion (given by T.H. Attwater of Lincoln's Inn) which the Committee had thought it prudent to obtain. This confirmed what was in fact obvious, that the university was not obliged to continue the chair. In counsel's opinion the furnishing of a 'Scheme of Work and Report' was 'an integral part of the bargain', which the university could not in propriety refuse to provide during the present tenure of the chair. The Professoriate Committee also reported that the following letter of resignation had been received from Toynbee, dated 6 December 1923:

> As I understand that at the Professoriate Committee yesterday it was questioned whether I had definitely resigned or not, I had better repeat that I have done so, without any condition (as I stated in my letter of 6th Nov[ember]) except to reserve my liberty to make a public statement if and when my resignation is accepted, as I assume that it will be accepted.

At the Senate meeting the recommendation, approved by the Finance Committee and the Academic Council, that, on the expiry of Toynbee's tenure, the endowment be returned, was withdrawn following the tabling of a motion proposed by Lord Justice Atkin and seconded by the Rev J.A. Douglas, two of Toynbee's principal adversaries on the Senate.[76]

Sir Gregory Foster, the Provost of University College, subsequently gave Eumorfopoulos, who was, of course, a colleague, a more informal account of the Senate's deliberations. Lord Justice Atkin in a speech, which in Foster's view had made a deep impression, had pointed out that the Senate had accepted the original conditions and that the Committee was only exercising its rights. It appeared to him that Toynbee's actions and words went beyond the right to freedom of speech and of conscience. He had asked, 'supposing Englishmen endowed an English chair in the Athens University, to which a Greek was appointed – supposing during the Great War, at the moment of England's greatest peril, this man had started a campaign against England – what would you have done?'. Atkin, seconded by Canon J.A. Douglas, had moved an amendment that the matter be referred back to the Academic Council. Professor Graham Wallas, on the other hand, had made a 'virulent' speech in support of Toynbee and had intimated that he thought Toynbee was right. This had brought a riposte from Professor Gardner. The extremist faction, led by Wallas, wished to return the endowment and terminate the professorship. They were against accepting Toynbee's resignation which they held would imply a censure of him. The Chairman of the Academic Council had made a feeble speech and the Academic Council's report had been withdrawn. Foster subsequently told Eumorfopoulos that, at the same meeting, Sir Wilmot Herringham had made an angry riposte to a speech in defence of Toynbee. This had begun, 'If the freedom of a professor means the liberty to be a cad ...'[77]

After the meeting of the Senate, although his resignation had not yet been formally accepted, Toynbee was anxious to secure an agreed statement from Barker which could accompany his own when his resignation was made public. On 21 December he wrote to Murray that he had had a long and rather hammer-and-tongs, but none the less friendly, and in the end not unsatisfactory, interview with him. With Murray's help, which Barker welcomed, he was sure that it would be possible to find a formula that Barker could accept. Toynbee apparently drafted a statement for Barker to sign. This made the point that he had twice offered to resign and that, indeed, when Barker had discussed the position with Toynbee and a small group of colleagues in the autumn of 1922, Toynbee had again suggested that he should resign and stand for re-election. Much emphasis was laid on the fact that 'by an unfortunate oversight' Toynbee had never been made aware of the various conditions attaching to the chair. Barker by no means agreed to accept Toynbee's draft wholesale and this last point was, more-over, omitted from the letter, the draft of which Barker sent to Toynbee on 26 December before discussing it with him and Murray. This was the version printed as an appendix to Toynbee's letter to *The Times* of 3 January 1924, in which he made public for the first time the fact that he had submitted his resignation.[78]

In his letter to *The Times*[79] Toynbee wrote that during the course of a visit to the Near East he had felt it his duty to comment publicly 'in a strongly unfavourable sense' on the conduct of the Greek armies in Asia Minor. He had since given free expression to his opinions as these had developed, exercising a freedom which he believed to be his right as a professor in a British university. From the beginning, however, he had been aware that his stance might affect the interests of the college and university and he had therefore immediately told Principal Barker of his readiness to resign, if at any time the situation became too embarrassing for the college and university. He added that he was deeply appreciative of Principal Barker's kindness and that he much regretted the trouble he had caused him by action of his which he had believed it right to take. In fairness to himself and to the donors he felt that he must also state that for nearly two years after raising the question of his resignation with the Principal he had remained unaware that the donors had retained any legal control over the endowment. He then went on to outline the conditions that had been attached to the endowment. Through an 'administrative oversight' these conditions had not been made public either in the advertisement for the chair or in the terms of appointment and he had only learnt of them during the fourth year of his tenure. Nor had Barker been aware of these conditions until the same time. Specific enquiries at the time of his candidature in 1919 had not brought them to light. 'Had I learnt of them,' he concluded, 'on the day of my appointment I should have withdrawn, in order to follow another career which was not at that time closed to me. Had I learnt of them at Yalova, in Asia Minor, on May 24 1921, I should have done precisely what I have done since then.' A concluding quotation 'from a very much more eminent historian [Polybius] than myself who, more than 2000 years ago, took a similar view to mine of a similar situation' was not printed, although *The Times* at this period did from time to time print Greek tags in Greek characters. This read as follows:

> Καιτοι τινες ισως επιτιμησουσιν ημιν ως φιλαπεχθως ποιουμενοις την γραφην, οις καθηκον ην μαλιστα παντων περιστελλειν τας των Ελληνων αμαρτιας ... συγγραφεα δε κοινων πραξεων οθδ' ολως αποδεκτεον τον αλλο τι περι πλειονος ποιουμενον της αληθειας.
>
> (And some may perhaps consider me as writing in a hostile vein; it being my duty [as a Greek] to cover up all the faults of the Greeks ... [But] in a chronicler of public affairs in no wise is anything other than the truth acceptable, Polybius, *Histories*, Book xxxviii/4)

Barker's letter to Toynbee of 26 December was appended to Toynbee's letter. Barker began by saying how sincerely he regretted the severance of Toynbee's connection with King's for he had done everything in his power to aid the college. He confirmed that, from the middle of 1921 'when you were absent on leave in order to study on the spot, in Greece and in Asia Minor, the subjects of your chair', Toynbee had always contemplated the possibility of resignation. He had not suggested that Toynbee resign because it had been his desire not to interfere with the freedom of opinion and expression of a professor of the college. 'I need hardly add,' he concluded, 'that the high regard which I have always entertained for your scholarship made me reluctant to contemplate the possibility of the step which you have now felt bound to take.'

Once Toynbee had gone public over the issue of his resignation, it was inevitable that the press, newspaper and periodical, should take up the case. On 5 January Glasgow argued that the fact that Toynbee's original offer of resignation was sent from Asia Minor, before he knew anything of the conditions attaching to the chair, demonstrated that the conditions had nothing to do with the question of his resignation. For the rest, it was a matter of personal taste, about which there could be no argument.

Mr Toynbee was the first occupant of a Chair established for an academic purpose on a Greek foundation, and for the greater part of his time has engaged in violent political propaganda against Greece. It is not a question of liberty of opinion.

Moreover, the endowment of university chairs by foreign bodies was no new thing. If, for instance, the professors on the Rockefeller endowment at University College were to spend their time not in teaching medicine but in engaging in political propaganda against America, their position would be untenable.

Liberty is not licence. Mr Toynbee had every right to attack Greece at any time, if he thought fit to do so; but the moment he started to do so he ought surely to have decided not to accept another penny of Greek money. If he had resigned in 1921 the case would have been different.

The fact that Toynbee had learnt of the conditions attaching to the chair only in the fourth year was, Glasgow argued, a testimony to the restraint of the donors. Glasgow's letter would have appeared on 4 January had not the editor of *The Times* placed it in his pocket before he went out to dinner and only got back to the office when it was too late for that night's edition.[80] One correspondent wrote to Gennadius on 5 January to say that the following passage had been omitted from Glasgow's letter: 'Mr Toynbee actively contributed to a Greek disaster, one of the most tragic in Greek history, and was able to do so precisely because of the prestige he derived from holding the Greek chair'.[81] To Glasgow's letter Toynbee sent a reply insisting that it was an issue 'not of personal taste but of principle'. But this was held over by *The Times* and on 8 January Toynbee informed the paper that he would prefer that the letter was not now published.

Most press comment was sympathetic to Toynbee. The *Yorkshire Observer*, for instance, came out on 4 January in support of Toynbee and denounced London University as 'a stronghold of Grecophilism', while the *New Statesman* on 5 January declared that 'the fault seems to rest with London University, which did ill service to the cause of University education by accepting an endowment under conditions utterly alien to English University traditions ... Nor can one greatly blame the Greek donors; for they only exercised a right which the University was careless enough to concede'. The *Manchester Guardian* of 14 January reported that Harold Laski had spoken about the case at a meeting of the University Labour Federation at Toynbee Hall and had urged that universities should not accept endowments under such conditions as had led Toynbee to losing his chair. The *Nation and the Athenaeum* on 12 January came out with a powerful and anonymous, albeit not wholly accurate, editorial in Toynbee's favour. This stated that Toynbee had initially declined to become a candidate in part on the grounds that in chairs 'founded by the natives of particular countries for the study of those countries there was sure to be an element of propaganda, which would be incompatible with the necessary freedom of the Professor's teaching'. On this point he had received the emphatic assurance that 'once the foundation had passed from the hands of the donors into the University no element of propaganda remained. The Professor was just as free as any Professor of Russian or Chinese or Ancient Icelandic. Thus reassured, Mr Toynbee became a candidate for the Chair and was elected'.

The editorial went on to describe Toynbee as 'an historian and scholar of unusual brilliance' whom it would be utterly unfair to describe as anti-Greek.

> He wrote and spoke in favour of the return of Cyprus and the Dodecanese to the Greek nation; he was active in trying to obtain help for the Greek refugees; he wrote clearly and pointedly on the injustice done to Greece in the recent dispute with Italy. But on the one great question about which all the emotions of Greece were aroused, the Koraes Professor pronounced against the beliefs and wishes of Greek patriots.

As soon as Toynbee learnt about the conditions attaching to the chair he felt he had no alternative but to resign.

> No complaint [the leader concluded] can reasonably be made against the action of the Greek donors, who, indeed, in view of the right of control which they had reserved, displayed considerable patience. But it is plain that the University of London should never have accepted their offer on such terms. It is an invariable and almost sacred rule in all self-respecting Universities that, when once money is given to the University for scientific purposes, it belongs absolutely to the University and the donor retains no control or power of interference. The present case shows the soundness of this rule, and the dangers which lurk in any departure from it. The deed makes provision that at the end of five years the donors may alter the terms, and the University, if not satisfied, may hand back the Foundation. It seems clear that one of these courses will have to be taken.

The force of this editorial was somewhat diminished by the fact that its author was Murray, as Toynbee's mother was somewhat disappointed to learn, as she had hoped it had been written by an outsider and dispassionate critic. 'Of course we will be secret; it would be injurious if it leaked out'.[82]

The Observer's London University correspondent, who was apparently Glasgow,[83] was distinctly unfriendly in an article of 6 January. Pro-Toynbee letters appeared in *The Observer* on 13 and 27 January. C.F. Dixon-Johnston, for instance, on 13 January congratulated Toynbee on preferring 'to sacrifice his position and emoluments rather than mislead his country-men by a silence enforced by foreigners'. On 27 January E.N. Bennett, late fellow of Hertford College, Oxford, was scathingly critical of the university for according 'to a body of foreigners' the virtual right to dismiss a professor because of his 'private opinions on political or international questions'. These received a dusty answer on 20 January and 3 February from the London University correspondent, who persisted in regarding the issue as one of taste. On 20 January he reported that Wace and Miller were being mentioned as possible successors to Toynbee in the chair. On 3 February he suggested that Wace would be prepared to accept the post and argued that the general feeling was that the appointment of 'so distinguished an occupant would go a long way towards redeeming the chair from the hectic atmosphere which had enveloped it so far'. He would be able to develop the school of Modern Greek 'on more academic lines'. On 3 February the editor declared the correspondence closed.

As soon as Toynbee's letter had appeared in *The Times*, both Murray and Toynbee's mother hastened to congratulate him. In Murray's view the letter, while not attacking anyone else, had put Toynbee completely in the right. '... If the Greeks give trouble there may be a case for my cutting in'. His mother thought that he had made his position 'so absolutely clear and unassailable, and yet so temperate and so skilfully avoiding the mention of Burrows'.[84] Hilda Johnstone, Reader in History at King's College, wrote to say that she had marvelled again and again at Toynbee's courtesy 'in the midst of what was often utterly unfair and irrelevant discussion of things you understand much better than the people who were talking about them'.[85] R.H. Tawney, the historian, wrote to say that he was disturbed by the principle involved and that it was clear that the university had committed a grave error of judgement in giving the donors any *locus standi*. He was therefore proposing to introduce a resolution at the next meeting of the Board of Studies in History for forwarding to the Senate. This resolution, to the effect that, 'in the interests of academic freedom and historical science', the University of London 'should decline to accept any endowment to which is attached either explicitly or by implication, the condition that any Professor or other Teacher of the University should express, or refrain from expressing, any particular political opinions' was duly passed at the Board's meeting on 25 January.[86] On 16 January Margaret Hasluck wrote to express her sympathy with Toynbee's position and to say that when the chair had been offered to her late husband (F.W. Hasluck) he had declined, ostensibly on the ground of health 'but the real reason ... was that he feared the Greeks would make him work politically for them and keep him in political bondage'. '... He loved them, you know, but he knew them and there was always a touch of indulgence in his love for them'. Astonishingly, a few days later Mrs Hasluck, a distinguished scholar in her own right who was subsequently to gain a reputation as an Albanologist,[87] wrote to Toynbee to say that she was thinking of applying for the chair, to which Toynbee replied that he certainly had no objection.

Two Muslims also wrote in solidarity. On 4 January Ameer Ali, a prominent Indian Muslim, wrote to express his admiration for Toynbee's stance. He added that he understood that Yusuf Kemal was coming to England and that, if he were wiser than Ismet, he might think it politic to establish a chair (presumably in Turkish studies) at King's College. On 8 January one Rifaat wrote, in an appropriately Ottoman spirit of resignation from the Club de Constantinople in Pera, to say that 'you lost your job for Turkey and I lost my job for England'.[88]

Far from being stilled by Toynbee's public and unequivocal announcement of his resignation, the controversy in the college continued to rage. On 4 January Seton-Watson wrote to Barker to say that he had been horrified to read Toynbee's letter in the previous day's *Times*. He had known that Toynbee was threatening to run amok but he had not been prepared for his treating Barker with such a lack of consideration and common decency. Those with whom he had discussed the matter at King's were also disgusted. Public controversy 'of the most regrettable kind' was almost inevitable and sooner or later Burrows' name would be dragged into it. Seton-Watson thought that Barker had let his good nature utterly run away with him for giving Toynbee such a testimonial as was published alongside his letter in *The Times*. 'I regard it as quite abominable of him to use such a letter and intend to tell him so: for it puts you in conflict both with the University and with the known facts of the case as we had discussed them towards the close of the term'. He was, he said, not alone in thinking that after such a public exhibition Toynbee's resignation should take effect at once rather than next July. 'For the moment the Greeks are showing greater restraint than might have been expected', but 'of course they cannot remain silent in the face of such a challenge'.

To this Barker responded that he had tried to do the right thing in the whole matter but that it had been very difficult. He thought that Toynbee had been indiscreet: 'I will even admit that he has been indecent; but he has worked hard for the College, and he is now in a sad position'. He had insisted from the beginning that he should make a public statement. Barker had begged him to wait as the matter was still *sub judice* and he was still professor until 31 July and had told him that he could say whatever he pleased when he had ceased to be a professor. Toynbee, however, had argued, and this was a view which had touched Barker, that he would soon be out of a job and that, unless he explained something of what had happened, then there was little possibility of his finding a new one. While he had declined to go into the matters of the existence and powers of the Committee, and of Toynbee's ignorance of these, Barker had agreed to write him a letter stating the exact sense of the words about resignation that Toynbee had used and that he had worked to the best of his ability for the College. Barker did not think that he had done wrong in writing such a letter to help a man who had lost his job, nor did he want to shed 'one atom' of the blame attaching to himself. 'Personally,' he wrote, 'I do not regret my action, or inaction, in the past. If I had put pressure on Toynbee, I should have done worse than I did by not putting pressure on him. I was in a dilemma, and I chose the less of two wrongs – the wrong of interfering with a professor, and the wrong of letting the holder of a Greek chair continue to attack the Greek cause.' He had begged Toynbee to leave the memory of Burrows alone and thought that he would. He was seeing Toynbee the next day when he would suggest to him that, now that he had spoken, peace was proper.[89]

Seton-Watson also wrote, on the same day, 4 January, to Toynbee to make his criticisms directly. In a draft of this letter he wrote that he was horrified by Toynbee's sudden plunge into public controversy and felt bound to warn him that he was not alone in regarding his action as 'an open declaration of war. Surely you must have realised that such action makes continued silence quite impossible for many of your friends who had hitherto disapproved but tried to patch matters up. You simply force us all to publish the full facts, and this cannot help your cause'. 'I am bound to add,' he concluded, 'that in my opinion you have shown an utter disregard for [the] interests of [the] University and College and [of] your own chair and have cruelly compromised Barker. It is exceedingly unpleasant to have to write like this, but I see no help for it.'

Toynbee replied on the following day:

> It was good of you to write, feeling as you do, before taking whatever action you intend to take. Personally I have always wished that full public light should be thrown upon the whole history of the chair and of my tenure of it, for I think the cause an important one, as you will realise from the fact that I have staked my material interests and my reputation on it.

His public statement had not constituted a sudden plunge. In two successive letters to the Professoriate Committee of the Senate he had expressly reserved the right to make it and had waited eight months until the issue between himself and the Senate had been resolved. But for an administrative oversight the facts about the conditions attaching to the chair would have been made public knowledge four or five years previously. In conclusion he asked whether Seton-Watson still wished him to preside at a lecture he was due to give at the Cavendish Club on 16 January. If this might prove embarrassing then he would get the Club to find another chairman, if not then he would be happy to continue. Seton-Watson replied that, in view of what Toynbee had written, he really did think it wise to get an alternative chairman. 'I am exceedingly sorry,' he concluded, 'but in my opinion you are simply asking for trouble, and I fear you don't realise what many of us at King's think about it all.'

Toynbee showed or sent Seton-Watson's letter to Murray who replied on 7 January:

> Seton-Watson must be a little mad. Your letter was as considerate both to the Greeks and to Burrows as you could make it. Do not let yourself be rattled, and do not answer letters more than you are compelled to. I can always be turned on, as a pro-Hellene and friend of Burrows, when further defence is wanted.[90]

On 4 January Burrows' widow, Una, wrote to Gennadius to say that after Glasgow's riposte to Toynbee had appeared in *The Times* a number of university people, led by Seton-Watson, were going to join the fray by writing to *The Times* on the university aspect of the matter and that they would, of course, be in 'our favour'. 'We are going to rub in the point about Toynbee's academic incompetence, and I think you will agree that it is better that this point should be made not by the Greeks but by Toynbee's fellow members of the University.'

It appears, however, that no such letter was written. The Subscribers' Committee also stood aside from public controversy. Eumorfopoulos considered Toynbee's letter to *The Times* to have been at once somewhat feeble and rather clever. It was not so much an attack on the donors as on the university for accepting an endowment that interfered with liberty of speech and conscience and tried to make out that the resignation was entirely due to political causes. Toynbee had purposely put aside all the Committee's statements about the inefficiency of the chair and 'the lamentable way in which the teaching had ceased to fulfil the wishes of the donors'. This was a point that should be brought out clearly when a letter was written. Gennadius cautioned, however, that the Committee should await developments.[91]

Seton-Watson appears to have enjoyed considerable and weighty support within the college, including that of Bernard Pares, the Professor of Russian history and head of the School of Slavonic Studies, and of A.P. Newton, the Rhodes Professor of Imperial History. The latter wrote to Seton-Watson on 14 January to say that he very much regretted the tone of the leader in the previous Saturday's *The Nation* (which had, of course, been written by Murray). Disguise it as may be, he added, there could be no doubt that Barker had committed a serious error of judgement in not advising Toynbee to resign in 1921. 'Toynbee's taste was deplorable in not resigning before he launched his strictures publicly and to my humble judgement his sense of what is fitting to any man of decency is – Well, you can supply the missing word.' Men had changed sides in the House before now for what seemed to them a great cause, but the best custom had been to resign first and make their statement afterwards.[92]

On 16 January a meeting to discuss the whole affair, at which Toynbee could put his case to his critics, was held in the college, although at whose instigation and under what auspices is not clear. At some stage it must have been mooted that no discussion would be allowed, for Pares on 14 January informed Seton-Watson that he had pointed out to Barker if there was to be no discussion then such a meeting could only make matters worse. The day before the meeting Barker, whose wife at this time was gravely ill, told Toynbee that he had received a letter of protest from Pares, suggesting that he should not refer to Burrows or to anything mentioned in his letter to *The Times*, but rather should explain his 'action as professor in regard to the Greeks since 1921'.[93] Glasgow, who had earlier supplied Seton-Watson with 'ammunition' for the onslaught on Toynbee, including a memorandum 'on the journalistic and political activities of Professor Toynbee', now sent him a note suggesting that his critics in the College should all turn up at the meeting and ask whether comments were to be allowed. If they were not, then they should ceremoniously walk out before hearing Toynbee's statement. 'Won't this be more effective than simply staying away? This is just a suggestion which I quite see may appear brutal, but my blood is up.'

No record of what must have been an extraordinary and painful meeting appears to survive, although what seem to be Toynbee's and Seton-Watson's notes for the encounter are preserved among their papers. It is clear that discussion of Toynbee's statement was, in the event, permitted, for two days after the meeting Pares wrote to Toynbee to say that he had been entirely wrong in his presumption as to Pares' argument. He had been surprised that Toynbee had not heard him say that it would be 'absurd that professors should go in and out of office like a barometer registering the rises and falls of governments. If ever this applied, it would apply in the case of a

Chair in my subject [Russian history]'. The question of the derivation of the endowment 'so far from being unessential has been the starting point of all criticism of your own action whether by me or others'.[94]

During these critical days in the controversy Gilbert Murray, although staunch in his support for Toynbee, whom he appears to have advised at every stage of the crisis, was manoeuvring behind the scenes to try to take some of the heat out of the situation. Following the publication of Glasgow's attack on Toynbee in *The Times* of 5 January, Murray had written to him to say that he no longer felt able to contribute a memorial note on 'my old friend Burrows' to Glasgow's memoir of the late principal.

> ... I think you will agree that it would not be seemly for me to contribute to your book after your public attacks on Toynbee, especially as he has consulted me and accepted my advice on all the important points connected with his tenure and resignation of the Koraes Chair.

Toynbee's letter of 3 January to *The Times* had been as considerate towards the Subscribers' Committee and towards Burrows as he or Murray knew how to make it. He was therefore 'a little surprised that any friend of Greece or of the University should wish to turn a painful incident, now finished, into a new and public quarrel'.

Glasgow replied two days later that he regarded Murray's letter as a disappointment in every way. It was not he who had turned a painful incident into a public quarrel but rather Toynbee by publishing his letter in *The Times*. Glasgow had wanted nothing better than to have the incident kept in the background, but once Toynbee had made a public statement then he could hardly expect to be given a free hand and not be answered by people who felt very strongly about his conduct. He was at a loss to understand Murray's claim that Toynbee had been 'considerate' both to the subscribers and to the late Principal. 'Toynbee did a grievous wrong to both.' Nor did Glasgow regard the incident as finished. Not only had Toynbee already been responsible for the withdrawal by the Greek government of the salary of the lecturer in the department, Lysimachus Oeconomos, but he had also endangered the future of the Koraes Chair itself.

> The Chair was Dr Burrows's pet creation, Toynbee owed his appointment to Dr Burrows, and the lack of consideration as well as of gratitude seems to be on Toynbee's side for not only jeopardising Dr Burrows's creation, but also for casting indirect aspersions on his benefactor who is no longer here to answer them.[95]

Murray seems to have replied suggesting a meeting with both Glasgow and Seton-Watson. For Seton-Watson subsequently wrote to Murray to point out that his own attitude in the matter was not merely an isolated one but was shared by a number of colleagues at King's, in particular by those working on more or less parallel lines with Toynbee. He therefore suggested an informal meeting, besides himself, with A.P. Newton, the Rhodes Professor of Imperial History and chairman of the Board of Studies in History, F.J.C.

Hearnshaw, Dean of the Faculty of Arts and head of the History Department, and Bernard Pares, Professor of Russian History and head of the School of Slavonic Studies. Toynbee's press campaign had turned into a frontal attack on the university and college and he did not want to say anything of which his colleagues would not approve. He himself had tried desperately to keep out of the dispute for he had shared a general reluctance at King's to attack Toynbee or do anything which might have injured him. But he now reproached himself for failing to take action. Had he moved 18 months ago then it might have been possible to dissuade Toynbee from his 'disastrous Turkophil campaign'. But he was 'making it impossible for us to remain silent indefinitely'. The precipitate action of the university and college in returning the money [they had, in fact, merely offered to do so] had resulted 'in an utterly false and illogical position'. For they were acting as though they were the aggrieved party when in fact it was the Greeks who were the injured party.

In Seton-Watson's view Toynbee's action had been 'altogether scandalous and unjustifiable'. For, 'at the supreme crisis in the fate of the Greek nation – probably without exaggeration the most decisive since Xerxes', he had 'plunged into a violent propagandist campaign in favour of the Turks'. There had been no pressure on him to become an advocate of the Greeks. If he did not approve of their claims then he had only to keep his silence and continue with his teaching. 'But it was utterly incorrect to agitate against the nation to which the foundation of his own post was due.' By allowing him, in the name of academic freedom, to continue his campaign without rebuke, the university and college had created 'intense resentment throughout the Greek world'. The situation that had now arisen had in fact proved an ample justification for the various stipulations on which the subscribers had insisted. The university, indeed, owed an apology to the Subscribers' Committee. As the public controversy dragged on this would 'obviously raise the whole issue of foreign donors, and the consideration due to their rights, wishes or say prejudices'. Controversy could be expected to have a discouraging effect on prospective donors of all kinds if they saw that the university was in breach of its undertakings and that it could be induced 'to change its policy without rhyme or reason'. 'Such action seems especially pitiful, in the present instance, because it is taken towards a *small* nation and in a minor subject of study.' He found it impossible to believe that the university would have acted in a similar way had, say, Spanish or Italian chairs been involved. In such a case the ambassadors and the Foreign Office would undoubtedly have intervened at an early stage. If the endowment were returned without regret or apology, and the Koraes Chair as a consequence destroyed, he would have no course but to protest publicly on three grounds: the interests of a subject closely allied to his own; loyalty to the memory of Burrows, with whom he had collaborated in the foundation of the chair; and, finally, loss of confidence in the continuity of university policy, 'which is an essential foundation to the whole activity of the School of Slavonic Studies'. 'I quite realise,' he concluded, 'that this might place me in an impossible situation but I do not see any way of escape.'[96]

Murray replied on 15 January that he had difficulty in accepting Seton-

Watson's invitation to meet with a number of King's professors for he had no *locus standi* for treating with people 'who would practically be representatives of the College'. What he had had in mind was a private meeting of three friends of Burrows and Toynbee to clear up misunderstandings. He added that he had found a good deal of Seton-Watson's letter to be entirely unintelligible. He was certain that Toynbee had never organized or contemplated a 'press campaign', still less any kind of attack on the university, college, Burrows or the donors. '... But it looks as if some step which he has taken, in all probability on my advice and with my full approval, has given rise to some extraordinary misinterpretation.' This was why he had suggested a private meeting.

Seton-Watson replied that he was quite prepared to have a meeting with Glasgow and Murray alone. He referred briefly to the meeting that had taken place at King's the previous day, 16 January, between Toynbee and other members of the staff. Speaking for himself, he regretted the meeting and when asked to speak he had prefaced his remarks by saying that he spoke under protest. Murray, in suggesting a time for the meeting with Seton-Watson and Glasgow, ended on a conciliatory note: '... the more I look at this business the clearer it seems to me that nobody is to blame. Everybody has behaved quite normally, except that both Toynbee and the Greeks have shown rather more patience and consideration than could have been expected.'[97] Glasgow gave an account of the meeting between the three, which took place on 29 January, in a letter of the same date to Sir Cooper Perry. According to Glasgow, Murray in the end admitted that certain things that had hitherto puzzled him had been cleared up and conceded that 'the talk about the "conditions" attaching to the Chair is all rot'. 'He apparently was under the impression that as a result of Burrows's carelessness, or something equally foolish, the University had accepted the Greek endowment under humiliating conditions. We pointed out that on the contrary Burrows had accepted battle with the Greeks on that very issue, and had won his point, with the result that the Greeks have no control whatever over the Chair or the Professor.' Some of the correspondence between Burrows and the Greek Committee, which Glasgow had been able to show him, had 'made him open his eyes rather wide'. The difficulty was, Glasgow concluded, that very few of those who expressed views about the whole business knew what they were talking about.[98]

Besides crossing swords on Toynbee's behalf with Seton-Watson and Glasgow, Murray was also engaged in private polemics with Mrs Burrows. She had written on 13 January to say that she could not understand how Murray could have advised Toynbee to initiate 'this horrible business in the Press' which could only lead to an attack on her late husband. 'This being so it seems a cruel and terrible thing to have done. It is like hitting below the belt – which is not done'. Toynbee had not been publicly attacked in any way and she and others had successfully done their best not to let the Greeks say anything in the press. As Toynbee had already resigned there was no need to protect himself by starting a public controversy.

Murray replied on the 16th that he found Mrs Burrows' letter very painful and that he felt sure she misunderstood the situation. It had been necessary for Toynbee to state the grounds for his resignation but both he and Toynbee had been in absolute agreement that the statement must be made in such a way as not to attack anybody and, in particular, to keep Burrows' name right out of the matter. Toynbee had not responded to attacks after the publication of his letter in *The Times* and, so far as Murray was aware, there had been no suggestion that Burrows was in any way specially responsible for the 'administrative oversight' that had undoubtedly occurred. So far as Murray personally was concerned he had two principal desires: 'one is regard for Arnold; the other, regard for Ronald, and I believe that Arnold feels exactly as I do'. Mrs Burrows replied on the 18th to say that, while she appreciated his conciliatory reply, what had really hurt her was Murray's refusal to contribute to Glasgow's memoir of her husband, for Glasgow had answered Toynbee's letter not as an opponent of Toynbee but as the representative of her husband's friends at King's and in the university. Moreover, Toynbee had not only written to *The Times* but he had been interviewed and had had his photograph in other papers. To her certain knowledge two further attempts to have a statement published had been refused by the newspapers concerned.[99] As for her husband's letter of 23 April 1919 to Toynbee it was not the Principal but the Registrar who notified a professor of the conditions of appointment. Moreover, such conditions as did attach to the chair were irrelevant: 'even if there had been no condition or wish expressed the situation that has now arisen would still have arisen owing to the peculiar and unfortunate circumstances of the Greeks and the Turks and the fact that Mr Toynbee was Professor of Modern Greek'.

To this Murray replied sharply on 22 January that he did not find himself able to contribute to a book whose author 'was at the time making aspersions on my son-in-law, which I believe to be totally unwarranted'.[100] It is pleasant to record that the breach between Murray and Mrs Burrows was subsequently healed for in 1932 Murray unveiled an inscribed display cabinet in Burrows' memory in the Burrows Library at King's College.[101] On the day on which she first wrote to Gilbert Murray, 13 January, Mrs Burrows also wrote to Cooper Perry to say that she was very worried that the letters appearing in the press would bring her husband's name into the Toynbee business. Although she had herself kept very quiet she now felt that she could hardly bear any more. She wondered therefore whether the university could not do something to stop the continuing controversy. She added that King's College had apparently lost the Koraes Chair file, which she well remembered as she did all her husband's filing and had handed over the file after her husband's death.[102] 'Mr Toynbee and his friends are concentrating on trying to prove that the University did a dishonourable thing, and it ought to be squashed by a responsible person or persons of standing.' Cooper Perry replied on 26 January that unfortunately he could see no way in which the university could be of direct help, although he was sure that with such good friends as Mrs Burrows had she would be well able to defend the late Principal's memory.[103]

Toynbee had sent (by hand) a copy of the original of his letter to *The Times* to Cooper Perry on the day of publication, 3 January. Toynbee explained that he had not posted it the previous day because *The Times* had not been certain whether it could be printed in full. 'As you will remember,' he added, 'I reserved to myself the liberty to make a public statement in the letter in which I sent in my resignation to the Professoriate Committee of the Senate, and I see no reason for delay.' Due to the complexity of the university's administrative machinery his position had unavoidably remained *sub judice* for eight months (from May to December 1923) and neither the Senate nor himself contemplated any disposal of the Koraes Chair which would involve his continuing to hold it.

> As between the University and myself, there is therefore nothing further to be decided, and it is only owing to an administrative oversight that the facts in regard to the terms of endowment were not made public four or five years ago.

Cooper Perry, in his reply of 9 January, acidly observed that Toynbee's letter to *The Times* had reached him after he had already had an opportunity of seeing it in print. 'As you are aware,' he continued, 'the matter is still *sub judice*, and in these circumstances you will probably agree with me that it is better that I should not offer any comments upon your letter.'[104]

On the day following the publication of Toynbee's letter, 4 January, George Glasgow had written to Cooper Perry to draw attention to Toynbee's 'comic performance' and to point out that his own letter would appear on the following day. He wished that Cooper Perry had been in town the previous day as he had wanted to ask him what he thought of Toynbee's letter which, in his view, succeeded in letting the university down pretty badly 'and to that extent will be embarrassing for his champions in the University, if he has any left'. 'You will not be surprised,' he wrote, 'to find that the Barker pendulum has again swung to the other extreme, and that he has now completely abandoned the line he took at the last meeting ... Dr Barker is going to America this month and will not be missed.' 'An interesting point,' he added, 'is whether Toynbee is now to continue his Professorship to the end of the session having burst out in this way in the "Times".' Many of his colleagues at King's College, he believed, were proceeding on the assumption that Toynbee had now finished, and was not going to wait till the end of the session before leaving. In which case the university would do well to reach agreement with the Greek committee and have 'a sound man such as Wace appointed as quickly as possible'. Meanwhile Glasgow looked forward to an early meeting with Cooper Perry. It is clear, in fact, that Cooper Perry thoroughly disapproved of Toynbee's, and indeed Barker's, conduct. In the hope of saving the chair, he had begun to put out peace feelers to the Subscribers' Committee immediately after the Senate meeting of 19 December 1923. On 21 December he had written to Gennadius suggesting an informal meeting to see if there was any way out of the 'miserable tangle' into which the affairs of the Koraes Chair had fallen, to which Gennadius replied thanking him for a letter 'conceived in a spirit which I hope will find a response in our Committee'.[105]

The outcome of this meeting appears to have been a draft letter prepared jointly by Cooper Perry and Gennadius for submission to the Academic Council, before being placed before the Senate, for eventual communication

to the Subscribers' Committee. This contained what Cooper Perry considered to have been a very mild censure of Toynbee, namely a reference to
the need, if the chair were to continue in existence, 'to devise safeguards
against the recurrence of such lamentable indiscretions as have imperilled
the continuance of a Chair so lately established by Greek friends of England
for the promotion of studies to which the Senate must ever attach very high
importance'. The Academic Council, however, struck out the reference to
'lamentable indiscretions', as Eumorfopoulos had feared it would.[106] Following this setback, Cooper Perry had written to express his regret to
Gennadius that the Academic Council had not seen fit to endorse their joint
text with its very mild censure of Toynbee. As the Academic Council was
largely composed of professors it was very difficult to persuade them to
censure a fellow professor. Nevertheless, he hoped that the Subscribers'
Committee would be prepared to accept the letter, as amended by the
Academic Council, for the termination of his appointment represented the
substantial censure of Toynbee. 'Personally,' Cooper Perry added, 'as you
must have gathered, my sympathies are altogether with the Subscribers'
Committee, and I can hardly conceive in the future any such unfortunate
conjunction of individualities as Principal Barker and Professor Toynbee.'
He entrusted that Gennadius' *'mitis sapientia* may exercise a calming effect
upon your colleagues on the Committee, and that out of these waves we
may, as the Greek poet observes, "see peace" '.[107]

Gennadius was not at all pleased with this development, writing to
Cooper Perry on 28 January that he could not conceal his disappointment.
For their draft letter, as now amended by the Academic Council amounted
to this, – 'that Mr Toynbee has voluntarily resigned (being tired and
disgusted with the whole business, as he and his friends represent), and that
the University has simply accepted a resignation which, indeed, he pressed
upon them'. Not only had the Senate allowed him to enjoy the emoluments
of the Chair for the full term of five years but it had found in his conduct
nothing to dissent or differ from. He did not find it possible to be a
consenting party to a solution which not only left Toynbee's 'flagrant
conduct absolutely unscathed' but also 'implicitly reflects a sort of censure
on the Committee'. He could not press on his colleagues the acceptance of a
text against which his conscience revolted and which would completely
stultify the course followed by the Committee. In the view of the Subscribers'
Committee a satisfactory solution would be some expression of regret on the
part of the Senate.[108]

After this setback Eumorfopoulos had discussions with his colleague Sir
Gregory Forster, the Provost of University College, as to a form of words
that might prove acceptable both to the Senate and the Committee. He
himself took the view that a very mild Senate statement as to Toynbee's
responsibility was acceptable but not any ambiguity as to the direction in
which this responsibility lay. Marchetti and Ionides, so he informed
Gennadius, had been prepared to drop the epithet 'lamentable' while
leaving 'indiscretions'.[109] Glasgow was among those who had been trying to
induce the Subscribers' Committee to accept the omission of 'lamentable' on
the ground 'that nothing further can now be expected from the University,

and that the Toynbee fiasco is not the sort of thing that is encountered twice'. The most important person to square, he believed, was 'our friend Mr G[ennadius]' who was inclined to rage.[110] In his letter of 26 January Eumorfopoulos passed on the information that the Metropolitan of Thyateira, the religious leader of the Greek Orthodox community in Britain, had heard from the Rev. Hilarion Basdekas that at one of his lectures Toynbee, à propos the Emperor Heraclius' campaign of 630 AD. to recover the 'Wood of the True Cross', had said, 'Fancy making war for a bit of wood'. 'The remark,' Eumorfopoulos believed, 'is not only deeply insulting but shows a lack of historical feeling that is truly surprising. After all, a historian should be able to represent to himself the feelings of the people of the age he is lecturing about.' Eumorfopoulos had subsequently confirmed the story directly with Basdekas. It was true, although Toynbee had referred to a 'piece' rather than a 'bit' of wood.[111]

At the Senate meeting of 30 January the Academic Council's letter, as amended, was discussed. Sir William Collins moved an amendment to the effect that the following passage be included in the Senate's reply to Toynbee:

> The Senate recognises that, having regard to the conditions attached to the foundation of the Chair, the Subscribers' Committee are fully justified in deploring the circumstances which have imperilled the continuance of the Koraes Chair.

After what one participant described as an acrimonious debate this amendment was passed by a majority of 16 to 12.[112] This represented a substantial, if somewhat qualified victory, for the anti-Toynbee faction. As the Rev. J.A. Douglas, a strong opponent of Toynbee, subsequently reported to Gennadius, the amendment was not quite what he would have wished, but he hoped that it would enable the chair to continue. 'I trust,' he added, 'that we have heard the last of this preposterous fellow.'[113]

On 31 January Cooper Perry wrote to Eumorfopoulos, as secretary of the Subscribers' Committee, to communicate the Senate's official reply to Eumorfopoulos' letter of 25 October on behalf of the Committee. This stated that Toynbee's resignation had been accepted, with effect from 31 July 1924, when his initial five-year term expired. In view of the vacancy arising it was open to the subscribers to state whether they wished to withdraw the endowment from the university's control. The Senate wished for a meeting with the Subscribers' Committee to consider the position. He went on to repeat the Senate's strictures against Toynbee, namely that 'having regard to the conditions attached to the foundation of the Chair, the Subscribers' Committee are fully justified in deploring the circumstances which have imperilled the continuance of the Koraes chair'. None the less, the Senate considered it essential if the Koraes Chair were to continue that 'the Professor should be placed under similar conditions to all other professors so as to be responsible only to the Senate as the supreme Governing Body of the University'. Subject to this condition, however, the Senate had 'every desire to secure that the maintenance of the Chair should encourage that interest in Hellenic studies and the Hellenic people which has always been the pride of English learning'.[114]

On the same day, Cooper Perry sent a copy of the Senate's letter to the Subscribers' Committee to Gennadius. In a covering letter Cooper Perry told Gennadius that the passage which had been added was 'intended to convey to those concerned the sympathy we all feel for our Greek friends in the trouble and deep annoyance which they have experienced through the behaviour of the first Koraes Professor, and for which it must be admitted that some blame lies with the University as the body in which King's College is incorporated'. Direct censure, 'however well deserved you and I know it to be', had been difficult for the Senate had never made a judicial inquiry into the offences against '*les convenances*' that had been alleged against him and thus Toynbee's defence, if any, had not been heard. But the additional passage was, he felt, an indication of some change of heart on the Senate's part. If the proposed meeting between representatives of the Subscribers' Committee and the Senate took place then he hoped that Gennadius would speak his mind freely 'for, indeed, you have been very badly treated and "wounded in the house of your friends"'.

The Subscribers' Committee, and Gennadius in particular, were by no means happy with the Senate's reply. They held that Toynbee had escaped any real censure and that the Senate's insistence that the chair, if it were to continue, must in future be responsible only to the Senate appeared to bear out Toynbee's case.[115]

On 31 January Edwin Deller, the Academic Registrar, sent Toynbee a copy of the Senate's official reply to the Subscribers' Committee. Predictably Toynbee, too, was far from pleased. Nor was Murray, who described the letter as 'a great disappointment, a cowardly and poor spirited piece of diplomacy'. Barker told Toynbee that he was unable to understand how the offending passage about the subscribers being justified in deploring the circumstances that had imperilled the chair had been included. He had not himself been able to attend the meeting of the Senate at which it had been inserted, as it had been held on the day before his wife's funeral.[116] Murray now wrote to Cooper Perry on 2 February on the subject of the Senate's letter to the donors. He was, he wrote, 'of course pro-Greek' in his general sympathies: 'but Toynbee is a close friend of mine, and has in many respects taken my advice throughout the difficult situation'. He had spoken with Toynbee and with Seton-Watson and Glasgow to urge in the interests of all concerned that there should be no public recriminations and he had hoped that the matter would die down after Toynbee's 'very considerate' letter of explanation to *The Times*. But the Senate's letter to the Subscribers' Committee had come as a shock, for it appeared to him to contain both *suppressio veri* and *suggestio falsi*. Were it to be published he did not see how he could counsel Toynbee to remain silent. 'A young man with his career before him cannot submit to misrepresentations at which you or I might shrug our shoulders.' If, on the other hand, the letter were simply a private document intended diplomatically to appease the donors then Toynbee need have nothing to say and the matter could rest. Toynbee had been in constant consultation with Murray about his original candidature for the chair. Murray clearly remembered Toynbee's reluctance to stand on account of his fears that the Greeks would have some control over the chair. With some exaggeration, he wrote that he recalled Burrows' 'repeated and emphatic assurances' that they would not. The conditions of appointment had been issued in an imperfect form and he well remembered the astonishment with which Toynbee and he had first seen them four years later. 'I do not wish to blame Dr Burrows,' he concluded, 'I can understand his action and believe he acted in perfect good faith. He had, after a long fight, persuaded the Greeks to give up so much that he felt as if they had given up all.' None the less, the fact remained that Toynbee had been misled by the university on precisely the point about which he was specially concerned. 'And now, when he resigns under painful circumstances, after admirable and devoted work, the post which he would never have accepted had he not been misled, the University does not even say a word of polite regret.' Murray, while apologizing for 'butting in', asked Cooper Perry to do what he could to 'soften the asperities of the situation', which he believed he could do with his tact and authority.

Cooper Perry, in his reply to Murray on 4 February, stressed that he shared Murray's view that no purpose would be served by public recriminations. Certainly the Senate had no intention of publishing the letter. 'Whilst the back of the University is broad and somewhat insensitive, any public reflections on the memory of the late Principal of King's College must bring his widow into the field with results that would be in every way deplorable.' He believed it unlikely that the Subscribers' Committee would wish to publish the Senate's letter which he believed to be quite as unsatisfactory to the subscribers as to Toynbee's friends. Moreover, he was most anxious that Toynbee's career should not be 'marred by a Press campaign of allegations and counter allegations, knowing by long experience how greatly a man is prejudiced by protracted controversy even when justice is altogether on his side'. As evidence of his desire to soften asperities he referred Murray to his official press release, sent to *The Times* and other newspapers after the Senate meeting. This had contained no note of blame and had merely stated that an offer by Toynbee to resign had been accepted with effect from 31 July 1924.[117]

Murray considered Cooper Perry's reply to be quite sympathetic and his advice to Toynbee, contained in a letter of 6 February, was that he would do better to say nothing more 'unless the University officially accuses you of arson, sacrilege and murder. You have really come off from a dangerous situation with flying colours'.[118] On the previous day, however, Toynbee had written to Deller, the Academic Registrar, requesting him to lay before the Senate 'a respectful, but definite and formal' request for an answer to the question:

> Do the Senate recognise that, having regard to the conditions attached to the foundation of the Chair, by which certain rights were assured to the Subscribers, Professor Toynbee is fully justified in deploring the circumstances which led to his acceptance of the Chair in 1919 without a knowledge of these conditions?

In his letter Toynbee noted that in the Senate's letter to Eumorfopoulos of 31 January mention had been made of the special 'conditions attached to the foundation of the Chair'. Toynbee wished to remind the Senate that these conditions had not been communicated to him either in the advertisement or in the terms of appointment of 1919, or by the University at any time since.

> In offering myself as a candidate and accepting appointment in 1919, I gave up á career in the Government service which was at that time open to me, and I did this after anxious consideration, and in the belief that the conditions attaching to the Chair had been fully revealed to me. Had I known what the full conditions really were, I should never have stood for the Chair.

He maintained that the Senate's letter to the Subscribers' Committee had made it clear that, at the end of his first five years' tenure, the Subscribers' Committee could have prevented his reappointment, although in the terms of his original appointment there was 'no indication that any party except the Senate had power direct or indirect to decide whether my appointment should be continued when the first five years' term had expired'.[119]

Cooper Perry was naturally alarmed at the prospect of further contentious debate. Accordingly he wrote to Murray on 8 February to say that as Murray would not have had time to get in touch with Toynbee before his 5 February letter had been written, he was asking Deller to hold the letter back in the hope that Toynbee might have second thoughts. On the merits of the letter Cooper Perry wished to say only two things. The first was that Toynbee was wrong, 'and definitely wrong', to assume that the Subscribers' Committee could have prevented his reappointment. Reappointment was purely a matter for the Senate and the powers of the subscribers with regard to withdrawal or modification would have only come into play had there been a vacancy. If Toynbee had been re-appointed there would have been no vacancy. The second was that, if Toynbee's letter were placed before the Senate, it would have 'the effect of galvanising into activity an agitation which seems now to be dying down'. He knew that Murray was no more anxious than he was to see a renewed outbreak of controversy.[120]

On receipt of this letter on 9 February, Murray telephoned Toynbee and suggested that Toynbee seek a meeting with Cooper Perry to discuss his letter of 5 February to Deller. In the light of this meeting, which took place on 13 February, Toynbee wrote on the same day to Cooper Perry asking him to confirm in a letter, which could be shown to the Subscribers' Committee, that the conditions attaching to the Chair had not been communicated to him either in 1919 or subsequently. In this case he would be happy to withdraw his letter of 5 February. He urged that all parties should refrain from publicizing these letters.

Cooper Perry promptly replied the next day that, in the light of this letter, he thought it right to place on record that when Toynbee had been appointed to the chair in May 1919 'the statement of conditions supplied to you did not contain any reference to the source of the endowment, nor to what in Counsel's opinion is to be regarded as "an integral part of the bargain"', that is to say the wishes of the subscribers as set out in their letter to Principal

Burrows of 24 April 1918. A copy of Cooper Perry's letter was also sent, as Toynbee had requested, to the Subscribers' Committee and apparently also to Gennadius.[121] Cooper Perry had himself already expressed the belief to Gennadius that neither the Senate nor the Committee would wish to publish, a view shared by Eumorfopoulos who found it 'much more dignified to treat Toynbee with the contempt he so richly deserves than to cause people to think that such an individual has annoyed us so that we feel annoyed even after he has been suppressed'.[122]

In a covering letter to Toynbee, Cooper Perry said that he was glad to have had the opportunity of a talk with him and believed that nothing but good could come of it. Certainly the friendly climate established at the meeting encouraged Toynbee to turn to Cooper Perry for advice a few weeks later when it was put to him that he should stand for the new chair of International Relations tenable at the London School of Economics. Since he had already been engaged by the British (later Royal) Institute of International Affairs to write a survey of international relations in 1924 he believed he would be one of the natural candidates as the post was part-time. He asked for advice as to whether he should stand.

> On the one hand, there may be strong personal feeling against me, in the Senate and other quarters of the University, over the Koraes Chair, which would make it undesirable for me to stand; and on the other hand, if I were to stand, I should only wish to do so on the understanding that, if elected, I should remain as free as any other private citizen to express my opinions publicly on political affairs.

Murray counselled against his standing for the new chair, for, if he were appointed, the opposition would be very strong. 'All Seton-Watson's party would feel themselves tricked and your position would be painful.'[123]

On 16 February the Subscribers' Committee met to discuss their answer to the Senate. Gennadius was unable to be present but there was a larger than usual attendance, consisting of Nicholas Eumorfopoulos, Ionides, Mitaranga, Marchetti and G. Eumorfopoulos. The result of their deliberations was embodied in a letter sent by Eumorfopoulos to Deller, the Academic Registrar. This insisted that the Committee's powers could in no way be construed as giving it control over the professor during his term of office. The Committee was particularly anxious to make this clear in view of Toynbee's recent 'appeals to the public press and his publication of an indulgence from the Principal of King's College'. The Committee was agreeable to a meeting of three of its representatives with three representatives of the Senate and expressed the hope that the Koraes Chair could be maintained.[124] The Subscribers' Committee meeting of 16 February was adjourned until the 23rd. When it reconvened it was attended by Gennadius, Ionides, Marchetti and Eumorfopoulos. Ionides put before the meeting a draft letter asking the university to return the endowment, arguing that to adopt any other course would be to place the Committee in a position of inferiority. The others present objected, arguing that this was not possible constitutionally as fewer than eight of the twelve members of the Committee were present. It was further argued that it was most unlikely that the Senate

would subsequently agree to the continuation of the endowment in any form
if such a policy was followed. The form of letter agreed at this meeting was
duly sent by Eumorfopoulos to Cooper Perry on 1 March.[125]

The letter began by remarking that the Committee was relieved to learn
that, by the wise decision of the Senate, the Koraes Chair would cease to be
occupied by Toynbee.

> They, therefore, find it unnecessary to revert to the anti-Hellenic
> propaganda persistently carried on by its occupant. They feel glad to
> know that they have now done with Mr Toynbee, as this was the very
> purpose for which they addressed themselves to the Senate.

They were gratified to receive from the Senate an admission of the justice of
their concern 'in view of the lamentable proceedings which imperilled the
continuance of the Chair'. While they would have preferred the Senate to
have made a formal enquiry into the circumstances, they appreciated the
difficulties facing it. Moreover, they took comfort from the 'weighty pronouncement' made before the Senate by one of its members 'an eminent
upholder of the majesty of British justice' (Lord Justice Atkin). 'That
pronouncement stands, and the generous words of that great jurist, en-
listing, as they do, the respect of all, ensure our abiding gratitude.' They felt
that the wording of the Senate reply of 31 January might lead ill-informed
persons to the conclusion that up to the present the Koraes Professor had
been responsible not only to the Senate but also to the Subscribers'
Committee. But this would be a complete misunderstanding of the agreement between the university and the subscribers. All that the Committee
had done had been to draw the attention of the authorities to certain
occurrences and 'respectfully to ask them whether they considered the
continued tenure of the Koraes Chair by Professor Toynbee' was 'compatible with the object of its foundation'. 'Any individual Greek – whether a
subscriber or not – might have acted in a precisely similar manner.' The
Committee had felt it all the more important to make clear their attitude in
the light of Toynbee's appeals to the public press and 'his publication of an
Indulgence from the Principal of King's College'. 'They would have thought
that the Professor's respect for English custom and for academic tradition
would have led him to abstain from public discussion of a matter still *sub
judice*.' They were pleased to accept the Senate's suggestion for a meeting of
representatives of both sides to consider the position 'with a view to averting
in future such regrettable complications as have occurred'. The Committee
hoped thus that 'the Koraes Chair will be maintained as an earnest of the
bonds of traditional friendship which exist between the two countries and a
living source of that intellectual culture which is the noblest legacy of
Hellas'.[126] In acknowledging receipt of the letter Cooper Perry stated his
belief that it would be better not to print the letter in full in the Senate
agenda lest it gave rise to a recrudescence of press activity, although he was
doubtless glad of a suitable pretext not to provoke the wrath of the still
significant pro-Toynbee lobby in the Senate.[127] This advice appears to have
been taken by the Committee.[128] At its meeting of 26 March the Senate gave

its blessing to further negotiations with representatives of the Subscribers' Committee.

The Senate meeting of 26 March effectively brought the story to a close as far as Toynbee was concerned. It had an odd sequel, however, in April when there was a further flurry of interest aroused by rumours that Toynbee had accepted a post at the University of Constantinople. These Toynbee sought to clear up in a letter to *The Times* which was published on 16 April. What had happened was that Youssouf Kemal, the Turkish minister in London, had written to him on 10 March to say that the Minister of Public Instruction of the new Republic of Turkey was anxious to engage the services of foreign savants. Toynbee was a natural choice for his name was *unaniment aimé et estimé dans mon pays tant par suite des services rendus à la cause turque que de l'éclat de votre enseignement dans les universités britanniques*. He asked, therefore, whether he wished to teach in Turkey and, if so, which subjects. Toynbee replied on 13 March that he was touched and greatly honoured by the minister's letter. He much appreciated this invitation not only on account of the friendly spirit in which it was offered but because of his own feelings towards Turkey and the Turkish people. He was currently engaged by the British Institute of International Affairs to write a survey of recent international relations. He might be offered permanent work at the con- clusion of this task, which he would almost certainly accept. But if he were not offered such permanent work, then 'the attraction which I feel in any case for the Ministry's generous offer would remain'. He therefore asked for the offer to be held in suspense for a year. Even if a permanent post should not prove possible then he would still like to visit Turkey at regular intervals ('say, for two or three months every second year') so as to keep in touch with the intellectual life of the country. On 21 March he wrote to the Turkish minister to say that, while he was not now in a position to accept the invitation, he still hoped to visit the country for shorter periods. On 30 March he wrote to Hussein Bey Efendi at Robert College in Constantinople to say that after much heart-searching he had had to turn down the Ministry's offer, which had tempted him strongly. A number of friends had, however, pointed out to him that if he accepted such a position then he would be 'written down, not by my personal friends, but by the world at large, as a confirmed 'Turcophil', with the result that anything I said or wrote about Turkey would be discounted'.[129]

Among Toynbee's papers is a draft letter to the Turkish minister which was never sent, suggesting that he lecture at the University of Constantinople between May 1925 and the end of March 1926 on the history of international relations and the history of relations between East and West. He suggested £1,200 tax free (almost twice his salary as Koraes Professor), plus travelling expenses, as a suitable stipend.

NOTES

1. Kitsikis, op.cit., p. 457.
2. Ibid., p. 457.
3. Toynbee to Seton-Watson, 21 Sept. 1920 (S–W).
4. University of London Senate Minutes, 1920, 255.
5. *A Study of History* (Oxford 1954) x, pp. 138–9; Cf *The Western Question*, pp. 148–152. It was also during, or possibly a few months before, his tenure of the Koraes Chair that, walking along Buckingham Palace Road, Toynbee found himself 'in communion, not just with this or that episode in History, but with all that had been, and was, and was to come. In that instant he was directly aware of the passage of History gently flowing through him in a mighty current, and of his own life welling like a wave in the flow of this vast tide', *A Study of History*, x, p. 139.
6. Archives of the Smyrna High Commission, Greek Ministry of Foreign Affairs, 1921. I am grateful to Victoria Solomonidis for making copies of these documents available to me.
7. Toynbee, *Acquaintances* (Oxford, 1967), p. 245; *The Western Question*, pp. 287–8.
8. In other dispatches to *The Manchester Guardian* Toynbee did not hesitate, not merely to report on events, but also to give his own views as to what the British government should and should not do. On 11 June, for instance, he warned against British co-operation with Greece to bring Ankara to reason. Such action would cause 'irreparable mischief in Anatolia and endless racial war between Greeks and Turks'.
9. *The Western Question*, pp. 269–70.
10. Ibid., pp. 158, 162, 156–7, 212, 147, 63, 183, 320.
11. Besides the *Western Question* Toynbee had written a number of periodical articles on the subject. These included 'The war in Anatolia', *The New Europe*, xv (1920), pp. 74–7; 'British Near Eastern policy', *New Republic*, xxxii (1922), pp. 165–8; 'The dénouement in the Near East', *Contemporary Review*, cxx (1922), pp. 409–18; and 'Great Britain and France in the East', *Contemporary Review*, cxxi (1922), pp. 23–31.
12. *Documents on British Foreign Policy*, first series, xvii *Greece and Turkey 1921–1922*, p. 425. I am indebted to Victoria Solomonidis for this reference.
13. Pencilled note by Toynbee appended to his letter of 6 May 1922 to Barker (T). The original of this letter of May 1921 does not appear to survive.
14. Ibid (T).
15. *The Western Question*, pp. xi–xii.
16. *The Nation and the Athenaeum* (26 Aug. 1922), for instance, called it 'a most valuable book upon one of the threatening problems now before the world'. 'One cannot call Professor Toynbee exactly a pro-Turk but still less in the present volume does he display the old pro-Greek sympathies for which some of us sacrificed a good deal in the past'. The *New Statesman*'s reviewer (16 Sept. 1922) was of the opinion that Toynbee was one of the few 'who have seen the Graeco-Turkish conflict in its proper perspective, with a judgement that is warped neither by the fanatical partisanship of the sentimentalists nor by the cynicism of the "practical politicians" '. It was, he considered, 'the most important contribution to the literature of the Near Eastern question that has appeared since the close of the great war'. Other reviews are listed in S. Fiona Morton, op.cit., p. 62.
17. Hove, 1922.
18. Ibid., pp. 45, 64, 21.
19. London, 1922.
20. London, 1923.
21. Ibid., p. 11.
22. King's College, Delegacy Minutes, 27 Feb. 1923.
23. *Western Question*, 2nd ed. pp. ix–xi, xiv, xvii–xviii.
24. (S).
25. These lectures were apparently postponed until the 1923–24 session as Professor W. Barthold of the Petrograd Academy of Sciences had been invited by the university to put on a course of lectures on a similar subject.
26. (S).
27. Barker makes no mention of the Toynbee affair in his *Age and Youth: Memories of Three Universities and Father of the Man* (London, 1953).

28. Barker to Toynbee, 31 Jan. 1923 (T).
29. Murray to Toynbee, 2 Feb. 1923 (T).
30. This should have read 'annual'.
31. University of London, Senate Minutes, 1923, 4021.
32. The Greek government in August 1923 forwarded a cheque for £1,000 to cover its obligations for the 1919–20, 1920–21, 1921–22 sessions and the first term of the 1922–23 session. It was subsequently found that the subvention had already been paid for the 1919–20 session, Barker to Caclamanos 25 Sept. 1923, Archives of Greek Ministry of Foreign Affairs. I have been unable to determine at what stage the Greek government subsidy to the department ceased. As late as 1926 Caclamanos, the Greek minister, was recommending that his government renew its grant for the teaching of Modern Greek, University of London, Senate Minutes, 1926, 19.
33. (S).
34: Pember Reeves to Eumorfopoulos, 26 Feb. 1923 (G).
35. (G).
36. Eumorfopoulos to Gennadius, 24 March 1923; Gennadius to Eumorfopoulos, 25 March 1923; Gennadius to Ionides, 24 March 1923; Eumorfopoulos to Gennadius, 26 March 1923; Gennadius to Eumorfopoulos, 27 March 1923 (G).
37. Gennadius to Ionides, 1 May 1923 (G). See also Marchetti to Gennadius, (in Greek) 3 May 1923.
38. (S).
39. This had presumably been drawn up by Gennadius, a noted and learned bibliophile.
40. Unless and until it was proved that it was the Turks and not the Greeks who were the incendiaries at Smyrna 'the presumption lies against the Greeks who are the convicted perpetrators of the arson in the interior'; A.J. Toynbee, 'The dénouement in the Near East', *Contemporary Review*, ccxxii (1922), p. 415. Toynbee was subsequently to change in mind on this point. Some nine months later he wrote that his final conclusion, based 'on a combination of evidence', was that 'in Smyrna city (as opposed to Smyrna Province) the Armenians and the Turks share the blame while the Greeks are probably innocent'. He had, however, seen at first hand plenty of evidence of Greek devastation in the interior; 'The truth about Near East atrocities', *Current History* xviii (1923), p. 545.
41. Eumorfopoulos to Shovelton, 12 May 1923 (S).
42. Presumably E.A. Gardner, Yates Professor of Archaeology at University College, London and a former director of the British School at Athens.
43. Murray to Toynbee, 16 May 1923; Murray to Barker, 17 May 1923; Mother to Toynbee, 30 May and 13 June 1923; Eumorfopoulos to Gennadius, 3 June 1923 (T)(G).
44. Barker to Eumorfopoulos, 30 May 1923 (S).
45. Minutes of Delegacy of King's College, 29 May 1923.
46. The Academic Registrar (Edwin Deller) to Toynbee, 13 June 1923 (T).
47. Barker to Toynbee, 26 June 1923 (T).
48. Cooper Perry to Barker, 17 Feb. 1923 (T).
49. University of London, Senate Minutes, 1923, 4021–2.
50. Cooper Perry to Eumorfopoulos, 19 July 1923 (S).
51. Barker to Eumorfopoulos, 19 July 1923 (S).
52. Deller to Toynbee, 11 Oct. 1923; Eumorfopoulos to Gennadius, 20 Oct. 1923 (T)(S).
53. Spender, *inter alia*, was the author of 'The resurrection of Greece 1821–1921', *Contemporary Review*, cxx (1921), pp. 152–9.
54. Spender to Eumorfopoulos, 23 July 1923 (S).
55. Eumorfopoulos to Gennadius, 18 Aug. 1923 (G).
56. Eumorfopoulos to Gennadius, 20 Oct. 1923 (S).
57. For a detailed study of this episode, see James Barros, *The Corfu Incident of 1923: Mussolini and the League of Nations* (Princeton, N.J., 1965).
58. *Journal of Hellenic Studies*, xliv (1923), pp. 82–3.
59. Eumorfopoulos to Gennadius, 20 Oct. 1923; Mitaranga to Gennadius, 12 Oct. 1923 (S)(G).
60. Eumorfopoulos to Gennadius, 22 Oct. 1923 (S).
61. Eumorfopoulos to Cooper Perry, 25 Oct. 1923 (S).
62. Toynbee to Barker (draft), ? 6 Nov. 1923 (T).

63. Wallas to Cooper Perry, 15 Nov. 1923; Toynbee to Wallas, 18 Nov. 1923 (U).
64. Whether the School should have called the chair after a living statesman, at this time the President of the newly established Czechoslovak Republic, is a moot point. When, in 1976, a chair of Modern Greek studies was founded at Harvard University with an endowment from the Greek government it was named after the poet George Seferis, the brother-in-law of the president of Greece at the time it was instituted, Constantine Tsatsos. But at least Seferis had died some years before the chair was instituted. Incidentally, the subvention for the Seferis Chair, unlike that for the Koraes Chair, appears never to have been voted in the Greek Parliament.
65. These figures are taken from the draft of a document prepared by R.W. Seton-Watson for circulation to possible donors (S–W).
66. Titulescu to Barker, 4 Dec. 1923; June 1924; Seton-Watson to Wickham-Steed, 7 Oct. 1924 (S–W).
67. Barker to Toynbee, undated (probably 24 Nov. 1923) (T).
68. This was based on Burrows' private papers which had been donated by his widow to the Greek Legation. Whether these papers have survived and, if so, their present where-abouts, is uncertain. Like Burrows, Glasgow was a committed admirer of Venizelos. He was the author of a popular interpretation of Sir Arthur Evans' discoveries at Knossos, *The Minoans* (London, 1923) and of an Anglo-Hellenic League pamphlet on *The Janina Murders and the Occupation of Corfu* (1923).
69. Undated draft of letter from Seton-Watson to Barker (S–W). There is no doubt that Seton-Watson sent the letter to Barker. As it is in draft form I have silently expanded contractions, inserted definite articles, etc.
70. Barker to Seton-Watson, 16 Nov. 1923 (S–W).
71. Barker to Toynbee (undated, probably 24 Nov. 1923); Toynbee to Barker, 27 Nov. 1923 (T).
72. Eumorfopoulos to Gennadius, 25, 26 Nov. 1923 (G).
73. Barker to Seton-Watson, 9 Dec. 1923 (S–W).
74. Gennadius to Eumorfopoulos, 16 Dec. 1923 (S).
75. Barker to Toynbee, 9 Dec. 1923 (T).
76. University of London, Senate Minutes, 1924, 1141–5. These minutes were deleted from the copy of the Senate Minutes circulated at the time to King's College and presumably elsewhere.
77. Eumorfopoulos to Gennadius, 20 Dec. 1923 and 7 Jan. 1924 (G). Caddishness in this matter clearly lay in the eye of the beholder. On 5 February 1924, for instance, C.F. Dixon-Johnson wrote to Toynbee to complain that Glasgow, Burrows' biographer and defender, was, besides being malignant, impudent and deliberately inaccurate, what he should call a cad (T).
78. Toynbee to Murray, 21 Dec. 1923; Barker to Toynbee, 26 Dec. 1923 and the draft of a statement apparently prepared by Toynbee for Barker (T).
79. This is printed in full in the Appendix.
80. Una Burrows to Gennadius, 4 Jan. 1924 (G).
81. Unidentified to Gennadius, 5 Jan. 1924 (G).
82. Mother to Toynbee, 14 Jan. 1924 (T).
83. Eumorfopoulos to Gennadius, 6 Jan. 1924 (G).
84. Murray to Toynbee, 3 Jan. 1924; Mother to Toynbee, 3 Jan. 1924 (T).
85. Hilda Johnstone to Toynbee, 3 Jan. 1924.
86. R.H. Tawney to Toynbee, 11, 14 Jan. 1924 (T); Agenda Board of Studies in History, 25 Jan. 1924.
87. See, for instance, her *The Unwritten Law in Albania*, ed. J.H. Hutton (Cambridge 1954).
88. Margaret Hasluck to Toynbee, 16 Jan. 1924, 21 Jan. 1924; Ameer Ali to Toynbee, 4 Jan. 1924; Rifaat to Toynbee, 8 Jan. 1924 (T). Rifaat may have been the Rifaat Bey who, as *kaymakam* of Alaşehir under the Greek occupation, had been deported, with other Turkish notables, for complaining of Greek outrages to a Western consul in Smyrna, *The Western Question*, p.290.
89. Draft of letter from Seton-Watson to Barker, 4 Jan. 1924 and Barker's undated reply (S–W).
90. Draft of Seton-Watson to Toynbee, 4 Jan. 1924 (abbreviations have been silently

expanded); Toynbee to Seton-Watson, 5 Jan. 1924; Seton-Watson to Toynbee, 7 Jan. 1924; Murray to Toynbee, 7 Jan. 1924 (S–W)(T).
91. Una Burrows to Gennadius, 4 Jan. 1924; Eumorfopoulos to Gennadius, 4 Jan. 1924 (G).
92. Newton to Seton-Watson, 14 Jan. 1924 (S–W).
93. Pares to Seton-Watson, 14 Jan. 1924; Barker to Toynbee, 15 Jan. 1924 (S–W)(T).
94. Glasgow to Seton-Watson, 11 Jan. 1924 and undated note from G[eorge] G[lasgow]; Pares to Toynbee, 18 Jan. 1924 (S–W)(T).
95. Murray to Glasgow, 7 Jan. 1924; cf. Murray to Toynbee, 7 Jan. 1924 and Eumorfopoulos to Gennadius, 11 Jan. 1924; Glasgow to Murray, 9 Jan. 1924 (S)(T).
96. Copy of Seton-Watson to Murray, January 1924 (S–W).
97. Murray to Seton-Watson, 15 Jan. 1924; Murray to Toynbee, 16 Jan. 1924; Seton-Watson to Murray, 17 Jan. 1924; Murray to Seton-Watson, 22 Jan. 1924 (S–W)(T).
98. Glasgow to Cooper Perry, 29 Jan. 1924 (U).
99. Seton-Watson in his letter to Barker of 4 January had reported that he had heard that Toynbee had given statements to other newspapers.
100. Una Burrows to Murray, 13 Jan. 1924; Murray to Una Burrows, 16 Jan. 1924; Una Burrows to Murray, 18 Jan. 1924; Murray to Una Burrows, 22 Jan. 1924 (S–W).
101. Huelin, op.cit., p.68. It is also pleasant to record that in the early 1930s Mrs Burrows married George Glasgow.
102. The file appears subsequently to have come to light again as the college's record of the whole matter is fairly full.
103. Una Burrows to Cooper Perry, 13 Jan. 1924; Cooper Perry to Una Burrows, 26 Jan. 1924 (U).
104. Toynbee to Cooper Perry, 3 Jan. 1924; Cooper Perry to Toynbee, 9 Jan. 1924 (U)(T).
105. Glasgow to Cooper Perry, 4 Jan. 1924; Cooper Perry to Gennadius, 21 Dec. 1923; Gennadius to Cooper Perry, 22 Dec. 1923 (U)(G).
106. Eumorfopoulos to Gennadius, 17 Jan. 1924. Professor Gardner subsequently informed Eumorfopoulos that the Academic Council had rejected the original form of the draft for it would immediately be seen as a censure of Toynbee; Eumorfopoulos to Gennadius, 24 Jan. 1924 (G).
107. Cooper Perry to Gennadius, 23 Jan. 1924 (U).
108. Gennadius to Cooper Perry, 28 Jan. 1924 (U).
109. Eumorfopoulos to Gennadius, 17, 26 Jan. 1924 (G).
110. Glasgow to Cooper Perry, 2 Feb. 1924 (U).
111. Eumorfopoulos to Gennadius, 26, 27 Jan. 1924 (G).
112. Eumorfopoulos to Gennadius, 31 Jan. 1924, reporting intelligence he had received from Professor Gardner; University of London, Senate Minutes, 1924, 1590. Among those supporting Toynbee were Sir William Beveridge and Professor Graham Wallas.
113. Douglas to Gennadius, 31 Jan. 1924 (G).
114. Cooper Perry to Eumorfopoulos, 31 Jan. 1924 (G); University of London, Senate Minutes, 1924, 1595.
115. Cooper Perry to Gennadius, 31 Jan. 1924; Eumorfopoulos to Gennadius, 14 Feb. 1924 (G).
116. Murray to Toynbee, 3 Feb. 1924; Barker to Toynbee, 4 Feb. 1924 (T).
117. Murray to Cooper Perry, 2 Feb. 1924; Cooper Perry to Murray, 4 Feb. 1924 (U).
118. Murray to Toynbee, 6 Feb. 1924 (T).
119. Toynbee to Deller, 5 Feb. 1924 (U).
120. Cooper Perry to Murray, 8 Feb. 1924 (U).
121. Toynbee to Cooper Perry, 10 Feb. 1924; Toynbee to Cooper Perry, 13 Feb. 1924; Cooper Perry to Toynbee, 14 Feb. 1924 (U).
122. Perry to Gennadius, 7 Feb. 1924; Eumorfopoulos to Gennadius, 13 Feb. 1924 (G).
123. Toynbee to Cooper Perry, 19 March 1924; Murray to Toynbee, 20 March 1924 (U)(T).
124. Eumorfopoulos to Academic Registrar, c. 16 Feb. 1924 (G).
125. (S).
126. Eumorfopoulos to Cooper Perry, 1 March 1924 (U).
127. Cooper Perry sought Lord Justice Atkin's advice in the matter of publication of the Subscribers' Committee letter in the Senate agenda, adding that he had no idea which of the members of the Senate had 'blabbed' about Atkin's speech. Atkin advised against

publication. Cooper Perry to Atkin, 10 March 1924; Atkin to Cooper Perry, 11 March 1924 (U).

128. Cooper Perry to Gennadius, 5 March 1924; Gennadius to Cooper Perry, 7 March 1924 (U); Eumorfopoulos to Gennadius, 8 March 1924. Eumorfopoulos reported that he had heard that Toynbee had an article in the current number of *The Nation* ('Jubaland and the Dodecanese', *Nation and Athenaeum*, xxxiv (1924), pp. 787–9, 8 March 1924) which advocated the return of the Dodecanese and Cyprus to Greece. 'Nearly all of those who are anti-Greek in Greece's relations with Turkey and Bulgaria make a show of impartiality on the above two questions'.

129. Youssouf Kemal to Toynbee, 10 March 1924; Toynbee to Youssouf Kemal 13 and 21 March 1924; Toynbee to Hussein Bey Efendi, 30 March 1924; Toynbee to Ramsy Bey Efendi, 30 March 1924 (T).

4 The Aftermath

Once Toynbee's resignation had been accepted by the Senate and the public controversy had begun to die down, negotiations began to get under way between the university authorities and the Subscribers' Committee as to how the chair might continue in existence. On 4 May 1924 Eumorfopoulos wrote to Cooper Perry that the Subscribers' Committee was 'desirous that the said Professorship should continue under the same conditions as here-tofore'. In reply Cooper Perry on 27 May put forward a number of what he described as informal proposals about the future of the chair. The essence of these was that the Senate was of the view 'the best way to carry out the objects we have in common would be for the fund [which would need supplementation by King's College] now in the custody of the University to be definitely made over the University under a trust deed'. If it were to continue, then the conditions attaching to the Koraes Chair would have to be the same as those attaching to all other professorships.

Eumorfopoulos was unhappy with this response.[1] Meanwhile, he had been having informal contacts with both Barker and Sir Gregory Foster. Over lunch at King's College, Barker had been more hopeful about the future of the chair. If it were to continue then Barker was anxious that it should be full-time so that, as Eumorfopoulos put it, the incumbent might 'explain the Greek point of view'. Barker had told Eumorfopoulos that, until he had learnt from the Subscribers' Committee, he had been unaware that Toynbee had been to Ankara about a year previously. He had been so busy that he had not studied the newspapers very thoroughly and he had given Eumorfopoulos to understand that 'under the circumstances it was perhaps unwise for him to have written to Toynbee the letter that the latter had quoted in the Times'. Barker had added that 'the letters in the Times with regard to Toynbee's professorship at Constantinople had affected him considerably, and that he did not intend to justify Toynbee any further'. On 15 April *The Times'* correspondent in Constantinople had reported that Toynbee had declared his readiness to take up a post in the Faculty of Letters of the University. Toynbee, in a letter published the following day, wrote to confirm that he had been approached in connection with such a post, an offer which he had greatly appreciated, but that he had declined in view of other commitments.[2] With Sir Gregory Foster, Eumorfopoulos had discussed the model established by the Committee on Scandinavian Studies with respect to the promotion of Scandinavian studies at University College.[3]

When Eumorfopoulos next wrote to Cooper Perry on 3 June he complained that the university's proposals were over-restrictive in seeking to limit the future role of the Subscribers' Committee to further fund-raising. He pointed out that the principal duty entrusted to the subscribers was to see 'that the objects of the endowment were carried out by affording such help and making such suggestions as our close connection with Greek affairs would enable us to supply'. He therefore suggested the setting up in connection with the Koraes Chair of a Committee similar to the Committee for the Promotion of Dutch Studies, established in connection with the department of Dutch Studies that had been founded at Bedford College and University College of the University of London in 1919. The role of the Committee for the Promotion of Dutch Studies was to advise the Senate, through the Governing Committee of University College and the Council of Bedford College 'generally as to the Promotion of Dutch Studies funds', and to take such steps as they thought fit from time to time to raise additional funds in connection with the furtherance of Dutch studies in the university. The Committee was made up of six Dutch representatives and six representatives appointed by University and Bedford Colleges.[4] Soon after Eumorfopoulos had written to Cooper Perry, Gennadius wrote to Eumorfopoulos to suggest that he put pressure on the members of the Subscribers' Committee to attend meetings to discuss the proposed revision of the terms of the endowment in view of 'the apparent indifference with which our previous communications have been received'.[5] On 10 June Eumorfopoulos wrote to the subscribers to report on the meeting between members of the three-man sub-committee (Gennadius, Eumorfopoulos and Marchetti) and of representatives of the Senate that had taken place on 3 May and to inform them that Barker had agreed in principle that, in future, there should be two Greek representatives on the Board of Advisors when appointments to the Koraes Chair were made. The members of the Subscribers' Committee seem in general to have been in agreement with the actions taken by its sub-committee, although M.A. Mitaranga wrote to Eumorfopoulos from Marseilles on 21 June to suggest that it 'should be explicitly understood that steps shall be taken to prevent a recurrence of Prof. Toynbee's scandalous behaviour'.[6]

On 4 July 1924 Cooper Perry replied to Eumorfopoulos that he was agreeable in principle to the Subscribers' Committee evolving along the lines of the Committee for the Promotion of Dutch Studies. He confirmed that the Koraes Committee, as the advisory committee was to be known, would in future have the right to nominate two representatives, members of the Greek communities, to the Board of Advisors for the Chair. On 31 August Barker wrote to Seton-Watson that negotiations continued to wind 'their slow length along'. 'What will be settled I do not know, and when it will be settled I do not know.' But he was inclined to think that there would eventually emerge a chair with a guaranteed salary of £800 per annum, 'which is a fine chair', and that this might be advertised during the following spring (1925). In view of this he asked Seton-Watson to acquaint A.J.B. Wace, until recently Director of the British School at Athens, with the current position, for Wace was 'obviously the best candidate likely to present himself, and if he can wait in faith, and the chair materialises, he is pretty sure to be elected'.[7] Eumorfopoulos had already written to Gennadius on 20 April that Wace, who appears also to have been an acceptable candidate from the point of view of the subscribers, was interested in the chair although Barker had informed him that the salary might be reduced to £600, which was below the university minimum. On 27 July he had further written to Gennadius to say that Wace had been offered a post at the Metropolitan Museum of Art in New York. Apparently, however, the offer of a post at the Metropolitan fell through, although Wace was now offered a job in Philadelphia.[8] George Glasgow wrote to Sir Cooper Perry on 17 October in support of Wace's candidature. Wace had been offered a post in America by the Philadelphia Museum but this he had not yet accepted as he preferred a post in England if he could get one. 'He is extremely keen on the Koraes Chair, but feels that he cannot risk the bird in hand, and if the future of the Koraes Chair is not settled at next week's meeting of the Senate, it is almost certain that Wace will not be a candidate.' Glasgow imagined that from every point of view Wace 'would be regarded as a Godsend for the Koraes Chair in present circumstances, because he would please the University on academic grounds and would please the Greeks on general grounds'. Cooper Perry replied on the following day that while the general position in regard to the Koraes Chair was distinctly hopeful he could not be certain when the vacancy might be filled. Moreover, he personally had not the least idea whether other candidates with claims as good as Wace's might not present themselves.[9]

While these discussions were proceeding, negotiations were also under way between King's College and the Romanian government over the proposed establishment of a post in Romanian history. On 7 October, R.W. Seton-Watson wrote to H. Wickham Steed to express his concern that the establishment of a lectureship in Romanian history per se would constitute a reversal of the established conventions of both the School of Slavonic Studies and the History Board, whereby the emphasis had been on teaching history on a regional, rather than on a country, basis: 'in other words the units are deliberately made big'. He believed it unfortunate that discussion had taken place between the Principal of King's College and Nicolae Titulescu, at that time Romanian minister in London and subsequently Foreign Minister and President of the League of Nations, during the absence of Pares, the main protagonist of the regional system, and of Newton, the chairman of the Board of Studies in History. It was no doubt perfectly natural, he believed, that 'the Roumanians should want, from a propagandist point of view, deliberately to separate Roumanian history from its context and present it by itself'. What was necessary, however, was to make the Roumanians 'take as "big" a line as the Greeks'. In the case of the Koraes Chair modern Greek had been combined with Byzantine history and the History Board had insisted that Toynbee ('before he ruined his position and nearly ruined the Chair by political propaganda') should cover in his lectures the whole of the Levant and Asiatic Turkey. At the height of the war a Chair of Dutch Studies had been created but this had later occasioned much trouble and when the Belgians had later offered 'a rival Belgian Chair' it had been rejected, with very unfortunate results. When the foundation of Seton-Watson's own chair, the Masaryk Chair of Central European History, was first being considered, the idea had been put forward that it should be jointly established by the Czechs, Jugoslavs and Romanians, although the underwriting of the chair had finally fallen to the Czechs alone. But it had been made clear to the Czechs that 'there could not be any question of a Chair of purely Czechoslovak History and that they must consent to the subject being greatly widened'. This they had agreed to and the purview of the Masaryk Chair had been defined as covering the whole Danubian and Balkan area.[10]

Agreement in principle that the Koraes Chair should continue in existence, that the conditions attaching to it should approximate to those governing the Chair of Dutch Studies and that the university would make up the professor's salary to £800 p.a. in order to attract good candidates appears to have been reached fairly quickly.[11] But negotiations over the fine print appear to have continued well into 1925. In a letter to Eumorfopoulos of 25 February 1925, Cooper Perry referred to an earlier request that had been made by the Professoriate Committee of the Senate that the names of the members of the Subscribers' Committee be annexed to the new agreement that was being negotiated with the university. What the Professoriate Committee had in mind was that, as the original members of the Subscribers' Committee died out, there would be no fresh nominations and thus it would gradually cease to exist. 'In their view there was a certain danger to the future happy relations of the University and the Greek community if the subscribers as a body, or a Subscribers' Committee, were kept in existence for all time with indefinite rights of criticism and interference in University matters.' The Professoriate Committee, however, felt such confidence in the present body of subscribers that they had no objection to their retaining for life the rights vouchsafed to them in the original deed. Cooper Perry asked Eumorfopoulos to make it clear if the subscribers' wish was that their committee should remain in existence in perpetuity. In his reply of 7 March Eumorfopoulos argued strongly that the Subscribers' Committee should have the right to renew itself. The Committee was already empowered to fill vacancies and its members felt that they had been 'placed by the Subscribers in the position of Trustees for the Fund, and doubt whether they would have the right to modify these conditions'. Perry replied on 13 March that, 'after much discussion', the Professoriate Committee had decided to give way with regard to the indefinite prolongation of the existence of the Subscribers' Committee.[12]

Although this represented a very significant concession on the part of the university, not all the members of the Subscribers' Committee were happy with the new dispensation. The main dissident appears to have been Alexander Ionides who, on 22 May 1925, wrote to confirm his viewpoint in writing to Eumorfopoulos, for he believed that his membership of the Subscribers' Committee had placed him in a kind of fiduciary position. He had become a subscriber because the chair had been originally founded at the instigation of Venizelos and 'the interest in Hellenes and Hellenic affairs over here [i.e. in Britain], was, owing to that statesman, very much in the ascendant'. From the beginning he had strongly objected to the endowment being made over unconditionally to King's College and for this reason a clause had been inserted in the original Trust Deed to the effect that the endowment would revert to the Subscribers' Committee in certain circumstances, in which case it would be devoted to the advancement of the interests of the Greek community in London. Since the foundation of the chair, the average attendance at Greek lectures had been a mere 1.5 and he had no reason to believe that there was any real demand for a teacher of

Modern Greek in London, nor had he any grounds for supposing that there ever would be. It seemed to him, therefore, that to maintain the chair would be a waste of money. He accepted that his viewpoint had always been a minority one and that he had no alternative but to accept the decision of the majority. Eumorfopoulos appears to have tried to convince him otherwise, for Ionides felt obliged to write to him once again on 4 June to restate his position. At the suggestion of Venizelos a fund had been subscribed with a view to getting Miller to take up a position as lecturer on Greek and Byzantine affairs at King's College. 'We all knew how to admire both Venizelos and the philhellene he suggested for appointment, and subscribed our money.' From the very outset it had been agreed that the endowment fund was to be one 'for purely Anglo-Hellenic interests'. The professorship had manifestly proved a failure, both in terms of the appointment of Toynbee, and in the low attendance at lectures. For this reason he was strongly of the view that the funds should be allowed to accumulate to endow a lectureship on the model of the Gifford lectures.[13] 'so that when any prominent Phil-Hellene is available the Funds wherewith to arrange such lectures would be forthcoming'. To advertise for a full-time professorship when there was no demand for Modern Greek would be a sheer waste of money.[14]

On 5 June 1925 the Subscribers' Committee met to consider the report prepared by its three-man sub-committee (Gennadius, Marchetti and Eumorfopoulos) which had met with the representatives of the Senate to work out a revised scheme for the Koraes Chair acceptable to both parties. Section 5 of the revised trust deed provided for the establishment of a Standing Committee for advisory purposes (to be known as the Koraes Committee) on which the subscribers would have four representatives. Under section 6 the functions of the Koraes Committee were stated to be the offering of advice to the Senate through the Delegacy of King's College 'generally as to schemes for the promotion of Modern Greek studies in the University and to take such steps as they may think fit from time to time for raising further funds for the promotion of such studies'.[15] Section 7 provided that the subscribers would be entitled to appoint two representatives to the Board of Advisors which would advise the Senate on the appointment of a new professor. These two advisers would be chosen from the four Subscribers' Committee representatives on the Koraes Committee. One would be deemed to be one of the four college representatives on the Board of Advisors and one would be deemed to be an Eternal Expert appointed by the university. The sub-commitee strongly recommended acceptance of the scheme, being of the view that the compromise was favourable as it was possible to obtain and that it was in fact satisfactory. The university had increased the endowment by an amount substantial enough to attract a good candidate.[16] The Subscribers' Committee, which would continue in existence, would in future have a considerable influence on the choice of the professor and would, moreover, through its representatives on the Standing Committee be able to give advice on matters appertaining to the chair.

The original trust deed had stipulated that the terms of the endowment could only be altered if at least eight of its 12 members agreed to such a change. Although Ionides forthwith resigned, the remaining 11 members gave it their unanimous approval. Some, however, such as M.A. Mitaranga, did so with reservations. Mitaranga was worried lest, in the future, the subscribers might be unable to increase the endowment to meet the higher costs of maintaining the chair. This might result in the loss to the original subscribers of the entire £16,000 that constituted the endowment fund. He therefore believed that it might be better to cancel the trust and remit the funds to the original subscribers on a pro-rata basis. 'At any rate it should be explicitly understood that the committee do not assume – neither individually nor collectively – any responsibility whatsoever for the maintenance of the Chair.' In another letter written at about the same time (June 1925) and also apparently from Mitaranga, he again insisted that no guarantee, moral or otherwise, be given that the Subscribers' Committee would raise fresh funds in the future, least of all from the 'foreign' Greek communities or from Greeks not living in England. He, for one, wished to state quite frankly that he would not undertake any such mission or mandate. If the endowment was to continue in existence then it should be explicitly understood that steps should be taken 'to prevent a recurrence of Professor Toynbee's scandalous behaviour', and that Toynbee's own candidature when the chair was once again advertised would be eliminated.[17]

On 25 June 1925, the Senate recommended the continuance of the Koraes Chair provided that it was subject to similar conditions as all other chairs and was 'responsible only to the Senate as the supreme Governing Body of the University'.[18] Edwin Deller, the Academic Registrar, accordingly wrote to Eumorfopoulos to inform him that the Senate had formally approved the revised scheme. On the same day Cooper Perry wrote to Gennadius with the same news and to thank him very heartily for all that he had done to bring to a happy conclusion 'a most troublesome and vexatious business'. On 28 June Gennadius replied that it was indeed a great relief to know the troublesome affair was over. Warm thanks were due to Cooper Perry for 'the consummate tact with which you have steered through many breakers'. He could appreciate his skill through his own experience, for he had had to get rid of Ionides who had been quite intractable.[19] The new trust deed regulating the Koraes Chair was duly signed by Gennadius on 13 July 1925. The following day Barker wrote to Eumorfopoulos that he had heard from the Academic Registrar that the university was now able to proceed to the election of a new Koraes Professor. The first thing that now needed to be done was to set up the Koraes Committee. He would see that the Delegacy of King's College appointed three representatives to the Committee and asked that the Subscribers' Committee should appoint four representatives of its own. Once instituted, the Koraes Committee could then appoint two representatives to act on the Board of Advisors for the chair. He hoped that it might prove possible for the new professor to take up his duties in January (1926).[20] The Delegacy appointed as the King's College representatives on the Koraes Committee Sir Israel Gollancz, Professor of English, Professor R.W. Seton-Watson, and J.A.K. Thomson, Professor of Classical Literature.[21] The four representatives of the Subscribers' Committee on the Koraes Committee were Gennadius, Marchetti, Mavrogordato and Eumorfopoulos, with Gennadius and Mavrogordato to act as the representatives of the Committee on the Board of Advisors.[22] Gennadius was to act as an External Expert, with Mavrogordato being regarded as a representative of King's College.[23] This, of course, meant that the subscribers retained a considerable degree of influence in the choice of Toynbee's successor, a substantially greater influence, indeed, than had been vouchsafed in the original terms governing the establishment of the chair. The Koraes Committee's membership was completed by Barker and by Sir Gregory Foster, now Vice-Chancellor. Once duly constituted, the Koraes Committee elected Barker as chairman and Eumorfopoulos as secretary.[24]

Once the Koraes Committee had formally come into existence, the way was clear for the election of Toynbee's successor. The Board of Advisors for the appointment included the Vice-Chancellor, Professor E.A. Gardner, Cooper Perry and Barker. The three nominees of King's College were Seton-Watson, Edwyn Bevan and John Mavrogordato. The three external experts were Alice Gardner, the Byzantine scholar, Sir Frederic Kenyon and Gennadius. Gennadius did not participate actively in the Board but concurred in its recommendation. Among those considered for the chair were H.J.W. Tillyard, the Byzantine musicologist, Lysimachus Oeconomos, A.A. Vasiliev, the Russian Byzantinist, Canon W.A. Wigram, the author of books on the Assyrian Christians, and F.H. Marshall, Reader in Classics at Birkbeck College, University of London, whose interests were largely focused on Greek history during the Byzantine and Ottoman periods. Marshall was duly elected and took up the post in October 1926. At Marshall's inaugural lecture the Greek minister, Dimitrios Caclamanos, discreetly referred to Principal Barker's 'efforts in overcoming some difficulties which have arisen with regard to the Chair'.[25]

The Subscribers' Committee continued in existence but as its members died, the remaining members decided not to fill vacancies as its only remaining function was to elect representatives to the Koraes Committee.[26] The Koraes Committee, which was presumably involved in the appointment in 1946 of Marshall's successor to the Koraes Chair, the Byzantinist R.J.H. Jenkins, survived into the 1950s. It was wound up in the early 1960s, when its last secretary, Peter Calvocoressi, handed the papers of the Subscribers' Committee and of the Koraes Committee to the Principal of the College, Sir Peter Noble, and was treated in return to a cup of tea and a pink cake.[27]

The formal demise of the Koraes Committee and the termination of its role in the selection of the Koraes Professor came in June 1961, when the Secretary of State for Education, under Section 18 of the Charities Act, agreed to the revocation of clauses 5, 6 and 7 of the revised Trust Deed of July 1925.[28] Only then did the university become fully sovereign in the matter of appointment to the Koraes Chair.

NOTES

1. Eumorfopoulos to Cooper Perry, 4 May 1924; Cooper Perry to Eumorfopoulos, 27 May

1924; Eumorfopoulos to Gennadius, 28 May 1924 (G).
2. *The Times*, 16 April 1924.
3. Eumorfopoulos to Gennadius, 18 May 1924; Eumorfopoulos to Gennadius, 2 May 1924 (G).
4. Eumorfopoulos to Perry, 3 June 1924 (S).
5. Gennadius to Eumorfopoulos, 9 June 1924 (G).
6. Eumorfopoulos to the members of the Subscribers' Committee, 10 June 1924 (G).
7. Cooper Perry to Eumorfopoulos, 4 July 1924; Barker to Seton-Watson, 31 Aug. 1924 (G) (S–W).
8. Eumorfopoulos to Gennadius, 20 April 1924; Eumorfopoulos to Gennadius, 27 July 1924; Eumorfopoulos to Gennadius, 12 Oct. 1924 (G).
9. Glasgow to Cooper Perry, 17 Oct. 1924; Cooper Perry to Glasgow, 18 Oct. 1924 (U).
10. Seton-Watson to Wickham-Steed, 7 Oct. 1924 (S–W).
11. Eumorfopoulos to Gennadius, 12 Oct. 1924; Perry to Gennadius, 27 Oct. 1924 (G).
12. Cooper Perry to Eumorfopoulos, 25 Feb. 1925; Eumorfopoulos to Perry, 7 March 1925; Perry to Eumorfopoulos, 13 March 1925 (S).
13. In ecclesiastical history at St Andrews.
14. Ionides to Eumorfopoulos, 22 May and 4 June 1925 (S).
15. One of the Greek members of the Koraes Committee, John Mavrogordato, was far from sanguine about the prospects of raising any further funds. As he wrote to Toynbee on 7 May 1924, the Greek community had been persuaded only '*with great difficulty* to subscribe to a literary and academic foundation instead of reserving all their money for political propaganda, and now not unnaturally feel that they have been let down. Never again, I can't help feeling, will an English University get an endowment of any sort out of the Greek community. (NB No Subscriber has said this to me. I am only guessing)' (T).
16. The amount of the endowment fund handed over to the university by the Subscribers' Committee was £16,031 7s 8d. The additional contribution by the university amounted to £4,736 16s 8d.
17. Mitaranga to Eumorfopoulos, 7 June 1925; ?Mitaranga to Eumorfopoulos undated June 1925 (S).
18. University of London, Senate Minutes, 1924, 3533.
19. Deller to Eumorfopoulos, 25 June 1925; Cooper Perry to Gennadius, 25 June 1925; Gennadius to Cooper Perry, 28 June 1925 (U).
20. Barker to Eumorfopoulos, 14 July 1925 (S).
21. Minutes of Delegacy, King's College, 28 Sept. 1925.
22. Mavrogordato had throughout the crisis managed to remain on good personal terms with Toynbee. In May 1924, after some kind of public row in which Toynbee had been involved, Mavrogordato wrote to say that he had regretted the painful scene. '... I think you know that I regard you as in effect, *but not in intention*, definitely anti-Greek, sometimes quite outrageously unfair to the Greek point of view'. None the less, the flagrant honesty of his intentions and the value of his work as an historian 'should be enough to secure you a reception in any civilized society', Mavrogordato to Toynbee, 7 May 1924 (T).
23. In a further concession to the Subscribers' Committee, the university agreed that the Koraes Chair, in respect of literary and linguistic studies, would henceforth be in the purview of the Board of Studies in Classics, and not, as hitherto, the Board of Studies in Oriental Languages. The Board of Studies in Classics would nominate the two additional 'external experts' in addition to Gennadius. Cooper Perry to Eumorfopoulos, 4 July 1924 (U), University of London, Senate Minutes, 1925, 4088.
24. Barker to Eumorfopoulos, 5 Oct. 1925; minutes of the meeting of the Subscribers' Committee 7 October, 1925; Eumorfopoulos to Barker, 7 Oct. 1925; Eumorfopoulos to Deller, 17 Oct. 1925; Eumorfopoulos to the Secretary of King's College, 17 Oct. 1925; the Secretary of King's College to Eumorfopoulos, 21 Oct. 1925; Deller to Eumorfopoulos, 21 Oct. 1925 (S).
25. King's College London Calendar for 1927–28.
26. Meeting of Subscribers' Committee, 26 Oct. 1932 (S).
27. Letter from Peter Calvocoressi, 8 Feb. 1982.
28. (K).

Toynbee's letter to *The Times* of 3 January 1924

THE LIBERTY OF PROFESSORS

MODERN GREEK CHAIR AT LONDON

MR TOYNBEE'S RESIGNATION

TO THE EDITOR OF THE TIMES

Sir, Having handed to the Senate of the University of London my resignation from the Koraes Chair of Byzantine and Modern Greek Language, Literature, and History, which is attached to King's College and in large measure endowed by donors of Greek nationality, I should be grateful for an opportunity to state briefly the facts of the position as far as they concern myself.

In the course of a visit to the Near East in 1921 I felt it my duty to comment publicly in a strongly unfavourable sense upon the conduct of the Greek authorities in the territories then occupied by Greece in Asia Minor; and since then I have taken every opportunity to study Greco-Turkish relations from both sides and have given free public expression to my opinions as the situation has developed. This freedom I believe to be my right as a Professor in a British University; and personally I should not be willing to hold an academic Chair under other conditions. It was obvious, however, that in the present case such action, though taken on my own responsibility, might affect the interests of the College and University, and therefore, by the same mail by which I dispatched from Constantinople my first articles to the English Press which were unfavourable to Greece, I wrote to Dr Barker, the Principal of King's College, explaining what had happened and what action I was taking, and informing him that I should be ready thenceforth to resign at any time if the situation became too embarrassing for the College and the University. For my relations with my College in the meanwhile I need only refer to the attached letter from the Principal (which he has kindly permitted me to quote), except to add that I deeply appreciate his kindness and regret the trouble which I have caused him by action of mine which I have believed it right to take.

In fairness to myself as well as to the donors, I must also state that, for nearly two years after I had first discussed with the Principal of King's College the question of my resignation, I still remained unaware that the donors had retained any legal control over the endowment. This fact was brought to my knowledge for the first time through the action of the donors themselves. In originally accepting the endowment the University had taken note that the donors were to be represented by a permanent committee, and had agreed that this committee should have a right to withdraw the endowment or to propose modifications in its terms whenever a vacancy occurred in the tenure of the Chair, the University retaining the right to surrender the endowment as an alternative to accepting any modifications proposed. The terms of endowment also embodied the expression of a wish by the donors that the holder of the Chair should submit to the Donors' Committee a programme of academic work at the beginning of every session, and a full report, with a request for criticisms and suggestions, at the end of every three years. By an administrative oversight these conditions were not made public either in the advertisement of the Chair or in the terms of appointment, and I learnt of them for the first time during the fourth year of my tenure. Nor was Dr Barker, whose connexion with the College began at a date subsequent to my own appointment, aware of these conditions until the same moment. I may add that specific inquiries which I made at the time of my candidature in 1919 did not result in bringing them to my knowledge. Had I learnt of them on the day of my appointment I should have withdrawn, in order to follow another career which was not at that time closed to me. Had I learnt of them at Yalova, in Asia Minor, on May 24, 1921, I should have done precisely what I have done since then.

I am, Sir, your obedient servant,

ARNOLD TOYNBEE

3 Melina Place, Grove End Road, N.W.8.

December 26, 1923

My Dear Toynbee, I am writing to say how sincerely I regret the severance of your connexion with the College at the close of this session. During the three and a half years in which you and I have been colleagues you have done everything within your power to aid the College, not only by your work in your own department, but also by voluntary and generous works of supererogation in the departments of History and Classics. I am grateful to you for the abundant services you have rendered; I am sorry these services must now cease.

While I am writing to you I feel that I ought to say (and you are entirely at liberty, if you desire, to quote what I say) that from the middle of 1921, when you were absent on leave in order to study on the spot, in Greece and in Asia Minor, the subjects of your chair, you have always contemplated the possibility of resignation. In your letter to me of May 6, 1922, for example, you wrote:- 'I should like to say again, what I wrote in my first letter about this business from Constantinople, that if ever circumstances, of which, in these cases, one is rather at the mercy, and of which one can never see the ramifications, should make it desirable, in the interests of the College and the University, that I should at any time offer my resignation, I should do that at once, and in fact should be grateful for a hint from you at the earliest moment that you felt that it should be done.' As you know, I have not suggested that you should offer your resignation, though I have again and again had anxious consultations with you, because it has been my desire not to interfere with the freedom of opinion and expression of a professor of the College. I need hardly add that the high regard which I have always entertained for your scholarship made me reluctant to contemplate the possibility of the step which you have now felt bound to take.

Yours ever,

ERNEST BARKER